Governing the Twin Cities Region

The Metropolitan Council in Comparative Perspective

The University of Minnesota Press
acknowledges with gratitude publication assistance
from the Roger E. Joseph Memorial Fund
for greater understanding of history and public affairs,
a cause in which Roger Joseph believed.

Governing
the
Twin Cities Region
The Metropolitan Council
in Comparative Perspective

by

John J. Harrigan
Department of Political Science
Hamline University
St. Paul, Minn.

and

William C. Johnson
Department of Political Science
Bethel College
St. Paul, Minn.

UNIVERSITY OF MINNESOTA PRESS □ MINNEAPOLIS

Library of Congress Catalog Card Number 78-3194

ISBN 0-8166-0838-5

The University of Minnesota
is an equal opportunity
educator and employer.

Preface

This book originated in the author's perception that after ten years of growth and activity, there is an unjustified lack of descriptive and systematic analysis of the Minneapolis-St. Paul Metropolitan Council. Aside from the Council's own publications, there has been little available for the citizen who seeks a comprehensive picture of its functions and policies. Likewise, urban scholars have not given the same analytical attention to the Metropolitan Council that they have given to the Toronto, Nashville, and Miami metropolitan governance structures.

As long as the Metropolitan Council operated quietly, behind the governmental "front lines"—the city, county, and state authorities —lack of attention, was, to some extent, understandable. But after 1976, when the Council was granted unprecedented powers over certain aspects of city and county planning, it became urgent to give this emerging power center some examination. There is also a strong movement, as of this writing, to make the Council a popularly elected body, and the Legislature has been confronted with that question in each of its recent sessions. Should the Council become elective, the authors believe this book will fill an urgent need for citizen information.

The authors have also noted that a re-examination of metropolitan governmental structure is again springing up in places such as

Denver, Detroit, Portland, and Rochester, New York. Although the political geography and policy patterns of every region are unique, and each region must create its own institutions, the experience of the Twin Cities area offers a helpful model. This model is not the Metropolitan Council itself but the process by which the area's needs were continually assessed and the policies and structures that were gradually built to respond to them. That process has been flexible enough to be sensitive to emerging public needs, yet consistent enough to permit stable policy to be formulated and implemented. It fits well with the American political culture's tendency toward incremental rather than radical change.

This project was immeasurably aided by many persons who provided information, resources, and criticism. First, the authors wish to thank the present and former chaimen of the Metropolitan Council: John Boland, Albert Hofstede, and James Hetland, Jr. Many current and former members of the Council staff added their contributions. Other persons contributed the perspectives of attentive outsiders. Two Bethel College students, Robert Haarsager and Brent Bostrom, researched particular topics to extend the authors' efforts. Kevin Harrigan helped organize the data for Table 5-2. The authors, however, take full responsibility for the facts and judgments presented.

John J. Harrigan   St. Paul, Minnesota
William C. Johnson   January 1978

Table of Contents

List of Figures

List of Tables

Acronyms and Abbreviations

Although the authors have minimized the use of acronyms in this book, it is impossible to follow the politics of metropolitan governance without some familiarity with acronyms. The following list is presented as a guide to terms that are commonly used in the Twin Cities.

A-95	The grant application process established by the Office of Managment and Budget Circular A-95
COG	Council of Government
DOT	Department of Transportation (federal)
ECSU	Educational Cooperative Service Unit (Minnesota)
EPA	Environmental Protection Agency (federal)
EQC	Environmental Quality Council (Minnesota)
HEW	Department of Health, Education and Welfare (federal)
HRA	Housing and Redevelopment Authority
HSA	Health Services Agency
HUD	Department of Housing and Urban Development (federal)
LEAA	Law Enforcement Assistance Administration (federal)

MAC	Metropolitan Airports Commission (Twin Cities)
MHB	Metropolitan Health Board (Twin Cities)
MHRA	Metropolitan Housing and Redevelopment Authority (Twin Cities)
MMCD	Metropolitan Mosquito Control District (Twin Cities)
MnDOT	Minnesota Department of Transportation
MPC	Metropolitan Planning Commission (Twin Cities 1957-1967)
MPCA	Minnesota Pollution Control Agency
MPOSC	Metropolitan Parks and Open Space Commission (Twin Cities)
MRA	Metropolitan Reorganization Act of 1974 (Minnesota)
MSFC	Metropolitan Sports Facilities Commission (Twin Cities)
MTC	Metropolitan Transit Commission (Twin Cities)
MUSA	Metropolitan Urban Services Area (Twin Cities)
MWCC	Metropolitan Waste Control Commission (Twin Cities)
911	A single emergency telephone number in the Twin Cities area
PPB	Planning-Programming-Budgeting
Section 8	A federal housing program for moderate income families
Section 208	An environmental planning provision of the federal 1972 Water Pollution Control Act
Section 235	A former federal housing program for moderate income families
Section 701	A section of the 1954 federal Housing Act that provided planning grants to regional agencies and local governments
SMSA	Standard Metropolitan Statistical Area
TAB	Metropolitan Council's Transportation Advisory Board
UMTA	Urban Mass Transportation Administration (federal)

Governing the Twin Cities Region

The Metropolitan Council in Comparative Perspective

CHAPTER 1

The Hope and Reality
of Metropolitan Reform

Governing a large metropolitan area is surely one of the more complex political problems facing a society. The typical metropolitan area in the United States is an intricate patchwork of community identities, governing institutions, and service systems. Lacking any central political authority, the region resists efforts to establish one — impressive testimony to the strength of the localist tradition in American politics. And metropolitan reform in such communities, when it has occurred, has often been at the initiative of the federal government, using its dollars as an incentive to get the local citizenry to do what it previously was unable or unwilling to do.

When a metropolitan area does succeed in organizing itself for effective planning, policy making, and coordination of regional public services, it is worthy of notice. Even more, it is worthy of study by those who seek to identify the key factors that made reform possible. This book is a study of one such extraordinary metropolitan reform — the creation of a system of governance for the Minneapolis-St. Paul Twin Cities region.

Should a diligent student try to find unique features of the Twin Cities area that could be pointed to as *the* determinants of this reform, only frustration would result. In most respects the area is typically midwestern in its economic base, ethnic stock, and political heritage. With a 1977 estimated population of 1,973,470, it makes up almost half of Minnesota's total population. The area is 3,000 square miles, and thus its density is 658 persons per square mile, quite low among large metropolitan areas. The population growth rate was high from 1950 to 1970, but it slowed considerably after 1970. The region's economy is strong and diversified. The unemployment rate is usually lower than that of the nation as a whole, and per capita personal income in 1974 was 13 percent higher than the national average.[1]

The region also has a large number of local governmental units, which is typical of midwestern metropolises. In 1977 there were 7 counties, 140 cities, 49 townships, 49 school districts, 6 metropolitan agencies, and 22 other special districts and agencies, a total of 273 governments.[2] If one also counts the 23 housing and redevelopment authorities, the total number of governments approaches 300. Few metropolitan areas have more governments.[3] The general-purpose local municipalities in Minnesota have a wide range of powers and function as healthy decision-making units for the most part. Neither this proliferation of local governments nor the tradition of strong local government has been conducive to metropolitan reorganization in other regions. On the contrary, as will be discussed later, these factors have usually been associated with the defeat of metropolitan reorganization schemes.

If there is any clear explanation of why the Metropolitan Council originated and how it has managed to function, it must be sought in the political conditions of the region. A number of factors have come together to establish a base of political support for the kind of governing institution that has received no warm welcome elsewhere. Leaders have appeared, from different sources and at different times, to take advantage of special circumstances. Although the authors cannot examine all the sources of these developments, they do wish to explain what these developments have been, how they have worked, and what fruits they have produced after ten years.

When the Minnesota Legislature established the Metropolitan Council in 1967, it designed an institution to take over the planning functions of the previously existing Metropolitan Planning Commission and to review local governments' applications for federal grants. Over the following ten years, the Council's role and authority have evolved to the point where the Council has now established metropolitan policies for a wide variety of public services. Moreover, it has acquired the power to secure adherence to certain of these policies by the other 272 governments in the metropolitan area.

This evolution of the Metropolitan Council's responsibilities has been unprecedented in American local government. All metropolises have been grappling with their area-wide governmental problems. The Twin Cities area has responded with a unique set of political institutions and processes that deserve analysis to determine both their effectiveness and their transferability. This book aims to provide that analysis of the Twin Cities' metropolitan governance system and, where appropriate, to compare that system with metropolitan developments in other regions of the United States and Canada.

In this chapter the Metropolitan Council is examined in the broader perspective of the metropolitan reform movement of the past thirty years. Four themes are significant for this examination. First, this period began with high hopes for creating general-purpose metropolitan governments that could improve public services and bring some order out of the governmental chaos that was thought to exist in most metropolises. Second, in most metropolises these hopes proved futile as they clashed with the forces defending the political status quo. Third, as these hopes were repeatedly dashed, the metropolitan reformers responded to the initiatives of the federal government by changing their emphasis from structural reform to improving the delivery of services and the quality of public facilities. Fourth, these federal initiatives, which came to stress coordination of the many urban policies, wrought a limited reform of metropolitan governing institutions.

The Great Hopes for Metropolitan Government

During the two decades following World War II, the political conditions of many metropolitan areas appeared headed for trouble, and the only way to deal with this seemed to be a radical restructuring of the area governments. One-third of the total American population lived in the megalopolises of the Northeast and Midwest.[4]

Most of the central cities there were ringed by incorporated suburbs and thus could no longer continue expanding through annexation of adjacent land. Of the metropolitan areas larger than a million people in the northeast quadrant, east of the Mississippi and north of the Ohio and Potomac rivers, 76 percent saw their central cities reach their population peaks by 1950 and decline steadily afterward. During these twenty years, there was a rapid increase in the number of suburban city incorporations and in special district creations. White middle-class people moved steadily from the central cities to the suburbs, and by 1970, nineteen of the twenty largest metropolitan areas had fewer people living inside the central cities than outside them.

This halt in central-city expansion and the rapid suburbanization of the metropolis led to numerous problems. The first was the inability of local governments to provide the normally expected urban services in suburban fringes. Critical problems developed in water supply and sewage disposal, for example. Since water and sewer lines were not extended into the new suburban subdivisions, homeowners had to rely on private wells and backyard septic tanks. This combination led, in the Twin Cities and elsewhere, to inevitable pollution of wells. Although it was often possible for cities or water supply districts to drill deep wells, it was much harder for a small community to set up a central sewage-treatment plant. In Jacksonville, Florida, the discovery that the St. Johns River was badly polluted from sewage was a factor in its city-county consolidation. In Nashville, Tennessee, the suburban communities' fire protection was provided by private companies. Residents subscribed for fire protection much as they purchased home insurance from a private insurance company. In the event of a fire, the chosen company would respond to a call and extinguish the fire. In one instance, a fire company arrived at the scene of a fire, not to put it out but to hose down the house next door. It had insured the neighboring house, not the one that was burning.[5]

Not only did the rapid suburbanization outstrip the ability to provide services, but it led to severe fiscal disparities among the metropolitan communities. There were wide gaps between the abilities of the central cities and their suburbs to finance needed public services, leading to significant differences in their quantity and quality.

Differences also appeared between individual suburbs. Some contained luxurious private residences and/or much commercial real estate. Others were lower-middle-class residential areas with little or no industry and shopping centers.[6] These disparities became highly visible in public education, where the school districts without luxurious homes or commercial real estate found themselves unable to provide all the educational services that the more affluent school districts could afford. Residents in the poorer districts began to file suits stating that such a method of financing education unconstitutionally deprived them of the equal protection of the law. This created a constitutional issue that each state now is seeking to solve in its own way.[7]

The typical metropolitan area displays a growth pattern that focuses commercial and industrial development along the freeways that radiate from the downtown district and encircle the region in "beltlines." This is characteristic of the Twin Cities region along Interstate Highways 35E, 35W, 94, 494, and 694. A few suburbs benefited financially from these geographic accidents, but most were left with an inadequate tax base. One result was a wide disparity in property tax rates from one community to another. A 1977 report by the Citizens League on such tax rates around the Twin Cities showed that the estimated tax on a house valued at $40,000 ranged from a high of $1,228 in Minneapolis (which also had the highest concentration of poor people) to a low of $607 in Eagan.[8] Even between some adjacent cities and school districts the differences were large. One's property taxes could vary by nearly $300 if one was on one side of a boundary line rather than the other. In effect, the quality of a child's education depended on the size of the tax base of the school district in which he or she was raised.

The most serious disparities in political terms were those between the central cities and their suburban areas as a whole. In most of the older and larger metropolitan areas of the United States, a dual migration occurred after 1945. Middle-class whites relocated to the suburbs. Less affluent persons, often racial minorities, migrated from the rural South to the central cities. This residential segregation was reinforced by the affluent suburbs' zoning practices. By requiring each new home to have a large minimum number of square feet, a garage, and a large lot, suburban officials could make the cost of homes beyond the means of low- and moderate-income people. This form of economic segregation has served to nullify for all practical purposes the fair-housing laws that were passed to attack the racial segregration those communities had long practiced.

As a result, central cities became overloaded with demands from persons who required more welfare services, health care, compensatory education, legal assistance, and police protection. One prominent urbanist characterized the old central cities of the Northeast and Midwest as "reservations" for the poor, the deviant, and the unwanted.[9] Another described them as "sandboxes" designed to keep their residents from causing political trouble, much as the backyard sandbox keeps children out of their parents' hair.[10] And one of the nation's major urban planners concluded that many inner-city neighborhoods and some entire cities were simply beyond redemption; they should be permitted to die.[11] No one has drawn a similar judgment about suburbia.

Although the central city-suburb disparities in the Twin Cities area were not as severe as in the older metropolises farther east, the problem was still present. Using 1970 census data, Edward Brandt showed that nearly 7 percent of Minneapolis and St. Paul families lived on incomes below the poverty level, but only one suburb had more than 3.4 percent in that category.[12]

Compounding the difficulty of resolving these fiscal and service problems was the fact that the typical governmental pattern in the metropolis was chaotic, a "nonsystem." In 1945, no metropolis in the entire nation possessed a governmental mechanism for dealing on a coordinated, area-wide basis with such problems as air pollution, sewage disposal, water supply, solid-waste disposal, mass transit, and public health which were beyond the abilities of any individual community to solve. Instead, the responsibility was divided among literally hundreds of governments. The New York City region was under 1,400 different local governments, the Chicago area under 1,100, and the Twin Cities metropolis had nearly 300. These figures included cities and villages, counties and townships, school districts, and special-purpose districts for such functions as sanitation, water, libraries, hospitals, transit, airports, and parks. Little attention was paid to coordinating the policies of these many units, and their activities often overlapped, conflicted, or left important gaps in service.

Thus, a four-lane divided highway might become a narrow street after crossing a county line owing to lack of intergovernmental cooperation, or an airport authority might plan a new facility on a site that would endanger urban water supplies.

A further consequence of this fragmented pattern of government was its lack of accountability to the public. It was hard for the average citizen, reading only the local newspapers, to learn which government was responsible for what functions and who was to blame for mistakes or lack of action. Different jurisdictions held elections at different times of the year, and the campaigns often received little media coverage. In the Minneapolis-St. Paul region, for example, the state elections are in November in the even-numbered years, school district elections in May of each year, suburban municipal elections in March of each year, some suburban township elections in February of each year, the St. Paul city election in spring of the even-numbered years, and Minneapolis city elections in fall of the odd-numbered years. In most metropolises, local candidates' records and platforms are hard to study and often deal with issues that appear trivial to most persons. When voter turnout for such elections is as low as it commonly is, officials of these units are chosen by those few with special interests in their actions. Although voters might occasionally refuse to reelect an office holder, they would find it hard to trace a relationship between that action and some resulting public policies. This dismal picture has generated considerable cynicism about the efficacy of local government, even while citizens continue to prize the "grass roots" values.

From the viewpoint of many political leaders in metropolitan areas, the only hope for dealing with this governmental chaos, the poor service delivery, and the unequal tax structure was to scrap the existing system of governance and create a single general-purpose authority at the metropolitan level. Their ideal strategy was the "one-government" approach, normally achieved by consolidating the central city with its overlapping or adjacent county. Its obvious advantage was structural simplicity and concentrating responsibility for public functions at one highly visible point. A single county-wide council would replace the previous city council and county legislative body, and the city and county service departments would be merged. The synthesis would prevent the formation of new municipalities in the suburban area and make special districts unnecessary. This re-organization was accomplished in Baton Rouge, Louisiana, in 1949, Nashville-Davidson County, Tennessee, in 1962 and Jacksonville-Duval County, Florida, in 1967. In addition, the city of Indianapolis, Indiana and Marion County were merged in 1969 by action of the Indiana Legislature, although the suburbs and special districts were left intact.

A second-priority strategy was the "two-government" approach.[13] This provided for local units to perform those functions deemed best suited to their scale, and a regional authority would be responsible for the broader functions such as sanitation, transportation, and regional planning. A charter would specify this division of powers and responsibility, with legislative bodies making laws at both levels. Toronto, Ontario, and Winnipeg, Manitoba, have instituted the "purest" form of metropolitan federation on this continent, and no United States region has copied them.[14] However, a slightly different approach to this was taken by Miami-Dade County, Florida. In 1957 the county government was reorganized with expanded regional service responsibilities for transportation, sewage, water supply, and land-use planning. The existing twenty-six municipalities continued to provide such local service as police patroling and zoning. Although more complex in structure than the first type and more open to conflict between the two levels, this approach has a political advantage in that it builds on an established foundation of local units and so would appear to voters and local elites as less disruptive of the status quo.

With one of these approaches in mind, leaders in many metropolitan areas devised specific proposals for submission to the voters in the popular referendum that was almost universally required by state law for major structural change. Generally, separate majorities in both the central city and the rest of the county or region were needed for passage. To be understandable to rank-and-file citizens and communicable in a mass campaign, the plans had to be simple, devoid of the exceptions and subtleties that the political realities might otherwise have dictated. Thus attention was focused on matters of structure and distribution of powers in a single major reorganization. Little or no provision was made for subsequent adjustment after the new system began operating, and the kind of political process and means of conflict resolution that would make the reform effective on a day-to-day basis was ignored.

The Great Hopes Dashed

From 1949 to 1974, forty-seven referendums were held on city-county consolidations, and only twelve passed. There were notable failures in such large metropolitan areas as St. Louis city and county, Missouri (1959), Cleveland-Cuyahoga County, Ohio (1959), and Portland-Multnomah County, Oregon (1974). Nearly all the other attempts, successful or not, were in the southeastern states from Virginia to Florida. The margin of defeat was usually large; less than 20 percent supported reorganization in the Knoxville and Chattanooga, Tennessee, areas.[15] The great hopes for reform were thus dashed to pieces under the steady blows of negative votes.

Several reasons for these failures were obvious. First, the reorganizations were heavily opposed by suburban voters in the counties to be consolidated with the central cities. They interpreted the reform as an attempted "grab" by central-city politicians of their tax base, schools, amenities, and, above all, their autonomy. A recent study indicates that their fear of increased taxes was the most important single factor in the defeat of many reform attempts.[16]

Second, these suburbanites, and many central-city residents as well, simply were not sufficiently dissatisfied with the existing governmental arrangements. Often, supporters of reform phrased their definitions of the problems in such abstract terms ("inefficiency" and "overlapping functions") that they had little meaning to the average person. Lowden Wingo has stated: "The conditions for political reform, then, require some critical mass of the unsatisfied. Lacking this, there is no logic strong enough to bring about the transformation, and that is what the gap between Utopia and Cleveland is all about."[17] The unknown is usually discounted in value in comparison to even a flawed present, and voters do not readily take risks with governmental structures.

Finally, the referendums drew opposition from many local elites who foresaw a loss in their own influence if they were approved.

All arrangements of governmental authority and functions can be seen as political games in which players gain, hold, and lose influence and resources. Whatever the rules are, they favor some contestants over others. A proposed change in the rules will clearly favor some, harm others, and leave a third group in an uncertain post-change position. Most likely, the latter two groups will join to defend the status quo; this is what happened with most of the reform referendums. Since the establishment of a centralized regional authority intentionally reduces the influence of leaders in the local units, their opposition was nearly unavoidable. At the same time, many ordinary citizens did not want to replace these local leaders, to whom they felt they had some access, with unknown metropolitan elites who might not be responsive to their interests. Considering these factors, it is surprising that any reforms were approved.

As urban scholars examined the evidence, it became clear that metropolitan reform succeeded only under unusual circumstances. Some were peculiar to the regions involved, and others depended on the political strategy and tactics used by the leaders of the efforts. First, most of the consolidations took place in the South, where metropolitan areas did not have a large number of incorporated suburbs or special districts. Thus, there were relatively few governmental centers of opposition to the plans.

Second, it was found that metropolitan reform would more likely be approved by voters if the campaign were waged as a "purification ritual," to use Scott Greer's term.[18] Greer distinguished that approach from the "capitalist-realist" campaign typical of the unsuccessful campaigns in St. Louis and Cleveland.[19] In the capitalist-realist campaign, proponents argued that the newly structured goverments would be more efficient and effective, eliminate duplication of services, and promote the growth of the metropolitan area. But such campaigns fail to excite voters, most of whom are not very concerned about forms of government or abstract questions of effiency.[20]

The purification ritual, by contrast, was used effectively in Nashville, Miami, and Jacksonville. In all three regions, political scandals had taken place which tainted the reputations of the leaders of the central-city governments. To a sufficient number of citizens, a vote for the reorganization was in effect a vote to throw the rascals out of office. In Miami, some police-department scandals had come to light just before the referendum, and Miami city officials were implicated in the wrongdoing. In Jacksonville, a number of city officials had been indicted for misusing their official positions. That they had not governed well was also apparent to the public, from the pollution of the St. Johns River and the loss of accreditation of the city's high schools. Nashville's successful referendum in 1962 had been preceded by a losing one in 1958. In the first campaign, the reformers had used the capitalist-realist appeal and aroused little voter support. In the intervening four years, the mayor of Nashville had initiated a very unpopular annexation of some suburban territory into the city. Further, the city had instituted a policy whereby suburban motorists had to buy and display a green sticker on their windshields if they wanted to drive their cars on the streets of Nashville. Voter support for consolidation rose by nearly ten percentage points for the second election.

A final factor associated with successful metropolitan reform efforts is the role played by local political elites.[21] They can have many reasons for either supporting or opposing the change—altruistic or selfish. But no reform plan has a chance for passage without advocacy by a broad spectrum of local leaders in government, business, civic groups, and the communications media. If these elites are either divided or united in opposition, they signal the voters that the plan is too uncertain or dangerous to deserve passage. Reform programs usually begin with the creation of a study or charter commission, involving some of the representative local elites, which then produces the specific plan. However, this kind of consensus is hard to establish over a short period of time. It develops best over a period of years in which a sense of metropolitan interests and a tradition of interlocal cooperation can grow. Of course, the sudden appearance of a crisis can stimulate elite agreement, if only because there is no workable alternative to reorganization, as in Jacksonville.

Those who sought to improve the governance of the Minneapolis-St. Paul metropolitan area were well aware of the fate of other regions' reform efforts and of the importance of understanding the unique local conditions. No city-county consolidation was seriously proposed, owing to the complexity of the local-government pattern. Metropolitan federation appealed to some leaders at first, but after visiting Toronto, they came back convinced that such an arrangement was not suitable for the Twin Cities. The lessons they learned centered on two basic points: (1) build a consensus around a set of principles that would meet the region's own needs, and (2) avoid a public referendum on whatever plan was proposed. The specific steps they took are the subject of Chapter 2.

The Public-Service Delivery Emphasis

While the voters were regularly rejecting metropolitan reform proposals, the problems they were designed to meet continued to worsen. However, help for these, and ultimate reform as well, was approaching from another direction. A common assumption by reformers was that each region was "on its own" as far as meeting its needs was concerned. The resources for dealing with the public problems of central city and suburb alike had to be drawn from within the region; hence the logic of a uniform metropolitan tax base for maximum flexibility in the distribution of wealth.

But the reliance on internal resources became less acute in the late 1960s. The emergence of Lyndon Johnson's Great Society administration saw a rapid proliferation of federal government programs to deal with metropolitan problems. The amount of federal money available for urban services was greatly increased. With these developments, the urgency of achieving metropolitan structural change lost some of its salience.

By the late 1960s, many urban reformers had stopped asking how metropolitan government could be attained. Now they were asking how the delivery of public services in metropolises could be improved. That question had a more feasible answer, though often not in clear or coherent form, in the growing programs of the federal government for urban aid. The Democratic administrations of Presidents Kennedy and Johnson could not ignore the problems of the cities—neither the housing and welfare needs of the central cities nor the environmental and transportation concerns of the suburbs. They took the initiative to portray to Congress and the nation these public-service issues as *urban* issues on which the nation had to take action in a comprehensive manner.

To be sure, federal programs of aid for urban areas had begun during the 1930s. Their purpose, through the 1950s, was to provide assistance to the state and local governments to achieve their own policy objectives, and to stimulate the construction of public facilities that were considered to be in the public welfare from both national and state perspectives. The majority of the funds went into such capital construction projects as hospitals, sewers, water-treatment plants, highways, urban renewal, and housing for low-income persons. By 1960, there were about 100 such categorical grant programs, supplying about 8 billion dollars to state and local governments. Much of it was spent in the nation's metropolitan areas, having been channeled through many state, county, and municipal administrative agencies and special-purpose districts. Most of these programs specified in great detail how the funds were to be spent, allowing the recipient governments little discretion in relating them to their own needs.

Under the Johnson administration, however, three major changes occurred in the purpose and direction of federal aid.[22] First, the emphasis switched from capital projects (which remained quite important) to the operation of human-service programs. This appealed to many previous advocates of metropolitan reform. If they could not restructure metropolitan governments to provide these services more effectively and equitably, perhaps the federal monetary incentives could improve these services. Thus, they lent their political support to the Great Society programs for income assistance, medical aid, compensatory education, job training, housing, and all the rest. For them, the federal income tax was proving to be the only way to draw wealth out of the suburbs for recycling to the central cities. In addition, it could redistribute resources from the richer regions to the poorer ones, crossing the state lines that were an impenetrable barrier to metropolitan reorganization.[23] Local leaders were quick to realize that federal aid was politically "free" in that they could enjoy increased revenue without unpopular increases in local taxes.

The second change in federal aid during the 1960s was simply in its magnitude. By the end of the Johnson administration in 1969 there were more than 500 grant programs funded with 25 billion dollars. By the end of the Nixon administration five years later, this had almost doubled to 50 billion dollars. Although some of this aid went to rural areas and nonmetropolitan communities, its thrust was still heavily urban. Naturally, the number of agencies involved in supervising and administering these programs increased also, compounding the problems of overlapping, conflicts, and lack of coordination.

Third, and most important, the priorities and core policies were increasingly being set by Congress and the federal agencies rather than being left to local choice. The federal grants were the key tools for implementing these new federal priorities. Essentially, federal funds constituted a network of incentives for state and local governments to achieve national goals, while the rules and restrictions accompanying the funds added a compelling mandate. Furthermore, the 1960s also witnessed new civil rights laws and court rulings that outlawed discriminatory practices throughout the public sector. Thus, under the combination of these policies, the federal government was obliging the cities and states to broaden housing opportunities, increase levels of public services to minority and disadvantaged citizens, and let the hitherto excluded segment of the population participate in local planning and administrative decisions.

From the viewpoint of metropolitan areas across the nation, these trends constituted a mixed blessing. There was often little cooperation between the agencies carrying out these projects, and programs for the same target population could work at cross purposes. The Minneapolis-St. Paul region experienced a number of such problems. Under a program supporting hospital construction, Twin Cities hospitals constructed far more bed space than was needed, which contributed to the rapid inflation of medical costs.[24] A related program stimulated rapid expansion in a nursing-home industry that spawned abuses which the state of Minnesota was soon forced to regulate. Finally, the Metropolitan Airports Commission, with access to federal funds, proposed to build a new airport on a site that the Metropolitan Council determined was unsound by federal environmental criteria. Naturally, the feedback to Congress from the state and local leaders who had to contend with these problems called for some remedy. They received it—in part.

Toward Metropolitan Policy Institutions

As examples of noncoordination proliferated with the growth in federal programs, it became apparent that not all the metropolitan reformers' goals had been fulfilled. Their "one-government" approach had been designed to bring order out of the intergovernmental maze, but that maze was strictly local in nature. Federal intervention had added even more players to the game and expanded the rule book considerably. Since the metropolitan areas were generally unable or unwilling to establish comprehensive authorities on their own, it was up to Washington to give them sufficient incentives to do so.

The first step toward this was taken in metropolitan transportation policy. Before 1962, federal highway programs had financed billions of dollars of freeway construction in urban areas, planned in complete isolation from questions of land use, public transit, and other important highway-related factors. In the Federal Aid Highway Act of that year, Congress stated that after 1965, highway funds would be supplied only to metropolitan areas which had a comprehensive transportation-planning process that could interrelate these factors. Under such an ultimatum, transportation study agencies were quickly organized in metropolitan areas, with inputs from local governments, state highway departments, and mass-transit agencies. Similar action was taken in 1965 to require a comprehensive area-wide plan before federal funding of water and sewer facilities.

A major step was taken in 1966 with the Demonstration Cities and Metropolitan Development Act, popularly called the Model Cities Act. Thereafter, applications by local units for federal funds had to be reviewed by an area-wide planning agency composed of elected local officials. It was to comment on the extent to which the local project was consistent with similar projects in other communities and with such comprehensive metropolitan plans as existed. These projects included hospitals, airports, libraries, water and sanitation facilities, highways, mass transit, land conservation, and open space. The comments of the reviewing agency, although not binding on the federal agency that supplied the funds, were intended to enable these agencies to judge the merits of the application in terms of local criteria. The precise guidelines for conducting this review were stated in 1968 in the Bureau of the Budget's (later the Office of Management and Budget) Circular A-95. Thus, these procedures are commonly referred to as the "A-95 review."

The basic intent of this review requirement was to create, and to endow with authority, institutions that could make policy for metropolitan areas as wholes. Many of the problems that the aid was designed to combat were of a large enough geographic scale that a regional approach was essential. But owing to the failure of the reform movements described above, few effective regional institutions existed in 1965. True, there were metropolitan sanitary, transit, water, parks, and airport agencies in many places, but these typically took as narrow a view of their responsibilities as did the highway planners. In fact, many federal regulations over the years had encouraged the creation of such special districts as a condition for financing those functions. But the policy coordination that Congress now demands calls for generalist institutions that can take a comprehensive approach to coordinating urban development for themselves. The general thrust of the A-95 procedures, as explained by the Advisory Commission on Intergovernmental Relations, is

to promote communication and coordination between generalists and specialists at all these governmental levels and to encourage an expanded decision-making process. . . . The circular itself cannot assure achievement of those objectives. It provides an opportunity for state and local governments to do so within their jurisdictions.[25]

Of this institution-building trend, Melvin B. Mogulof has concluded that

The repeated attempts of the Federal government to act with regard to metropolitan governing issues represents, in some fashion, an attempt to compensate for this lack of governing capacity at the metropolitan level.[26]

In response to these federal stimuli and in order to meet the undeniable problems that spawned the more radical reorganization proposals, there developed a trend toward voluntary interlocal cooperation through councils of government (COGs). A COG is a voluntary metropolitan body in which all the counties and municipalities are, or can be, represented. Typically, it consists of a representative assembly that adopts general policy on behalf of the member units, a staff that does research, planning, and policy implementation, and an executive committee that oversees the staff work. The council is financed by voluntary payments from each member and by federal government grants. Some COGs have been deeply involved in metropolitan planning and development issues, such as the Association of the Bay Area Governments in the San Francisco-Oakland region. Others exist simply as interlocal communication channels. No COG can require any government, member or not, to act against its will. Thus, it becomes very difficult to carry out projects that generate strong opposition, and the COG is limited to acting on matters on which a consensus exists.

The first COG was begun in 1957 in the Detroit metropolitan area, and by 1965 ten existed. Their numbers grew rapidly after the passage of the Model Cities Act of 1966, which had required some such area-wide agency to review the local application for federal grants. By 1970, there were more than 300 COGs. Although many of these, undoubtedly, only perfunctorily reviewed the applications, the potential exists for the council to exercise significant influence over metropolitan development. Yet its voluntary, nonstatutory nature makes it a fragile tool for making hard decisions.

At the substate level in Minnesota, regional cooperation since 1967 has been centered in thirteen regional development commissions. The Twin Cities metropolitan area constitutes Development Region number 11, and the Metropolitan Council is the most active and powerful of these substate bodies. The outstate commissions have run into formidable political opposition from local officials and until the last few years have been fairly impotent. However, as will be discussed below, federal government regulations and financial resources provide an increasingly powerful incentive for local governments to begin cooperating under the umbrella of the regional development commissions. As a consequence, these commissions can be expected to have a much more influential voice in the future than they have in the past. Perhaps the most active of the outstate commissions is the Arrowhead Regional Development Commission in economically depressed northern Minnesota. It performs many of the planning and review functions that are described in this book as functions of the Metropolitan Council.

The COG, the regional planning commission, and in Minnesota the regional development commissions have been aided by federal programs to assist comprehensive regional planning. Although planning grants had been made earlier to regional agencies under Section

701 of the Housing Act of 1954, this pace was increased after passage of the Intergovernmental Cooperation Act of 1968. Pursuant
to that act, part IV of Circular A-95 provides for channeling to regional agencies funds for planning transportation services, environmental quality, health care, community action, economic development, manpower, law enforcement, and services to the aged. These
planning grants have come to be the major source of funds for most
regional councils and commissions, and supply about half the revenue of the Twin Cities Metropolitan Council. Although this means
of financing is attractive to local officials, enabling them to finance
most COG operations from outside their own resources, it also provides potentially greater autonomy to the organization in choosing
its planning projects.

In conclusion, American metropolitan areas have passed through
two stages in the post-World War II process of building new governing institutions. The first stage, the establishment of self-initiated
structures for planning and delivering regional services, was aborted
in most areas because of political conditions that the reformers ignored or could not overcome. This experience led to efforts to re-
conceive the process in another womb—Washington, D.C.—and the
second stage built on federal government initiatives. These institutions have now come into existence, nourished by national authority
and funds, although their effectiveness in dealing with major metropolitan issues still leaves much to be desired in many areas. As a
result, federal agencies, and often those of the state government as
well, have become visible and powerful actors in the metropolitan
political process. Although their resources enhance and extend the
capabilities of local governments, they also limit the autonomy of
the local influentials and alter the rules by which they operate.

How These Developments
Impinged on the Twin Cities

All these developments impinged on the Twin Cities. The kinds of
problems in public services that affected Jacksonville, Nashville, and
Miami also affected the Minneapolis-St. Paul region. As will be shown
in Chapter 2, sewage-disposal problems and the wide-spread pollution
of the water supply created a severe crisis that had to be overcome.

The trend toward using federal grants to improve public service delivery resulted in a number of metropolitan agencies, special districts, housing and redevelopment authorities, and specific service programs that acted in isolation from one another to a considerable degree. Coordination of all these programs was clearly becoming a necessity.

The response of the Twin Cities regional decision makers to these conditions and stimuli was somewhat extraordinary among American metropolitan areas. Essentially, the two institution-building stages were telescoped into one. At the same time that the federal initiatives for reorganization were beginning to be felt, the efforts to establish a genuinely self-initiated and self-designed structure were strongest. The Minnesota Legislature was not willing to accept the council of government concept with its voluntary nature and domination by local officials. Those creative efforts have continued at a high level with the incremental growth and development of the Metropolitan Council. Chapter 2 chronicles and interprets the origin and evolution of this unique agency.

CHAPTER 2

The Origin and Evolution

of the Metropolitan Council

How did such an apparently ordinary metropolitan area produce so unique an institution as the Metropolitan Council? This question will be examined from several perspectives in this chapter. First, there are several political conditions in the region and in the state of Minnesota as a whole that are not so "ordinary" in their combination. These can be viewed as influential background factors in the Council's creation and growth. Second, a "metropolitan consciousness" had been slowly growing for forty years before the creation of the Council, and that consciousness did much to prepare the way for the Council. Third, the legislative act of 1967 establishing the Council was a major departure in policy, a *nonincremental* decision, in that it replaced a weak planning agency with a potentially strong policy-making authority that had no precedent on the American governmental scene. Finally, this chapter traces the subsequent evolution of the Council by means of a series of *incremental* legislative decisions that defined its nature and broadened its responsibilities. There has been much continuity in this pattern of development, remarkably so in the absence of a "master plan" for the Council's growth.

Favorable Background Features

There are four conditions in the Twin Cities' political ecology that appear to have facilitated metropolitan reform. None of them by itself has been *the* determinant, but without any one, the prospects for reform would have been much poorer. First, the obvious distinction that the region enjoys—two central cities and thus two growth nuclei—has minimized the rise of an overpowering "anti-big city" feeling among suburbanites. The two cities have long been rivals. To this day there is no genuine metropolitan newspaper, only St. Paul and Minneapolis papers. This rivalry has only recently been submerged in the growing need to cooperate on many problems such as sewage disposal, transportation, and protection of the Mississippi River shoreline.

A second important feature is that the Twin Cities region experiences little of the suburban distrust and antagonism toward the central cities that was detrimental to metropolitan reform in Cleveland, St. Louis, and a number of other areas.[1] Minneapolis and St. Paul share with their suburbs similar political styles and relative honesty in government. Like most of the older metropolises of the Northeast and Midwest, the suburbs tend to be more affluent than the central cities,[2] but the socioeconomic differences between the central cities and the suburbs are not as great as in many other metropolises.[3] There is more diversity between the suburbs themselves than between suburbia overall and the central cities. There are indeed serious disparities in fiscal capacity in the region. Minneapolis has the highest real-estate-tax rate in the region with a less-than-average per capita personal income to support it. However, some suburban communities and school districts have greater financial difficulties. As a result, the cleavages between the central cities and the suburbs have not been as detrimental to cooperation on regional service delivery problems as they have been in some other metropolitan areas. The people of the inner suburbs are becoming more socioeconomically similar to the populations of the central cities than they are to the outlying suburbs that are still growing and tend to be more affluent.[4] This may lead to future conflict between the central cities and inner suburbs on the one hand and the outer suburbs and rural areas on the other over the question of urban growth management. Some outer suburban officials complain that the Metropolitan Council is oriented toward the central cities to the detriment of their communities. In the 1977 legislative session, one bill was introduced to increase outer suburban representation on the

Council at the expense of the one person-one vote principle. Whether this potential conflict continues to grow or disappears will depend largely on how the Metropolitan Council makes use of its own powers.

A third relevant feature relates to the political culture and the high level of public services that the Twin Cities region has characteristically enjoyed. Daniel J. Elazar has labeled Minnesota's political culture moralistic, that is, one in which the state is expected to intervene in the economy for the achievement of social purposes.[5] Such a culture would support high expenditures for public services and extensive governmental innovation. Political scientist Jack L. Walker rated the states on the extent to which they adopted innovative ideas for programs and governmental structures and found that Minnesota ranked among the states most receptive to innovation.[6] These cultural factors appear to be reflected in Minnesota's level of public services. A recent survey by the Overseas Development Council of statistical indicators of physical quality of life placed Minnesota first in the United States and just under Sweden internationally.[7] Most of the indicators related to services for which government was partially or wholly responsible, such as health care and education. Minnesota is also one of the most heavily taxed of the states and has a highly progressive income-tax structure. From this evidence, it can be surmised that Minnesotans expect more from government, particularly from their state and local units, and will take a greater interest in how effectively those governments are run. This feature of Minnesota's political culture may stimulate a more positive climate for governmental reform than exists in most other states and metropolitan areas.

Closely associated with the political culture is a fourth distinctive feature of the Twin Cities metropolitan region—the existence of some broadly based, unifying civic institutions that participate forcefully and effectively in political decisions. Once organized on a separate St. Paul and Minneapolis basis, some important business, labor, cultural, and educational groups in recent years have come closer together on a wider metropolitan basis that reached into the suburbs. The local governments have organized into an effective Association of Metropolitan Municipalities distinct from the state-wide cities' group. A council of metropolitan area units of the League of Women Voters researches regional issues and makes recommendations.

Probably most influential, though, has been the Citizens League. It is a broad-based organization with members from all parts of the region that has operated with metropolitan focus since the early 1960s. Its primary activity is to support research committees on topics of public concern, in which its members voluntarily take part. After several months of study, a committee issues its findings and recommendations for policy, which is made public after approval by the League's Board of Directors. These reports are read carefully by decision makers, both because of their high overall quality and because many of the committee members have considerable expertise and political influence in their own right. Over the years, many major regional policies can be traced to an idea or an endorsement in a Citizens League report. These reports have covered not only the establishment of the Council but also such topics as mass transit, housing, land use, waste management, and environmental protection. The League is as nonpartisan as an influential civic organization can be and concentrates on pragmatic problem-solving rather than on ideological debates. Although many of its members are active in the Democratic-Farmer-Labor or Independent-Republic party organizations, the League itself does not endorse candidates for office. Its executive director, Ted Kolderie, and other professional staff members are well informed and maintain close contacts with business, civic, and political leaders in the area. With these resources, it can help mobilize significant influence behind its favored reforms.

The Growth of a Metropolitan Consciousness

The promoters of the Metropolitan Council in 1967 did not start from point zero. Rather, the reformers of the 1960s could look back on forty years of efforts to build a regional base for public policy. In 1927, a group of citizens organized a voluntary planning association for the metropolitan area. However, it lacked reliable financing and official support, and soon ceased operating. A more significant move was the creation in 1933 of the Minneapolis-St. Paul Sanitary District to cope with the pollution of the Mississippi River. It gradually expanded its operations in sewage collection and treatment until by 1970 it served forty-five suburban communities. Another unifying move occurred in 1943 when the Legislature resolved an intercity dispute over the location of a major airport by establishing the Metropolitan Airports Commission to develop and operate such facilities on a unified regional basis.

A vital step toward metropolitan unity was taken in 1957 when the Legislature organized the Metropolitan Planning Commission (MPC). The MPC's jurisdiction was extended in 1959 to cover the same seven counties as are in the Metropolitan Council's jurisdiction — Anoka, Carver, Dakota, Hennepin, Ramsey, Scott, and Washington. Twenty-three of the commission's twenty-seven members were chosen by or from the local governing units in the region. It was the first agency of its kind in the United States. The MPC's function was purely advisory, and it could compel no other unit to comply with its plans.[8]

Gradually, the MPC gained influence. A 1962 survey showed that the Twin Cities, along with Milwaukee, ranked first among large, midwestern metropolitan areas in per capita commitment of money and personnel to comprehensive planning.[9] After 1962, the MPC cooperated with the Minnesota Highway Department in the Joint Program, the transportation-planning process that Congress had required of states as a condition for receiving future federal highway grants. The MPC began to perceive that the location of freeways in the metropolitan area had a great impact on land use, and in its last four years it prepared a rudimentary *Metropolitan Development Guide* to account for the many growth stimuli and their consequences. Clearly, its work laid both a political and technical foundation for the subsequent accomplishments of the Metropolitan Council. At the same time, its very lack of power to implement its plans was a key point in the reformers' arguments for replacing the MPC with a more effective agency.

In general, the metropolitan agencies created in the 1940s and 1950s acted very competently within their individual jurisdictions, and they enjoyed a very positive reputation. But the creation of these agencies led many regional-minded elites to become concerned about a new problem — the proliferation of, and lack of coordination among, the special districts. The Airport Commission enjoyed substantial autonomy despite the great impact that its responsibilities had on the general development of the region. When a proposal to establish a metropolitan transit district came before the Legislature in the mid-1960s, many lawmakers opposed it. They feared that a proliferation of metropolitan districts would lead to the piecemeal development of regional governments without the means to relate each piece to the other or to any overall development plan. Leaders were clearly beginning to perceive a need for policy leadership at the metropolitan level which the Legislature was unable to give in its biennial sessions.

The coming of the Metropolitan Council was also hastened by the appearance of tangible evidence that the existing nonsystem of service delivery was becoming detrimental to people's well-being. The population of the Twin Cities suburbs grew by 115 percent during the 1950s, and this created pressure on water and sewer services. The new suburbs got their water by drilling deep municipal wells or by relying on individual home wells. The sewage problem, however, was not so easily resolved. The two central cities opposed expanding sewer facilities to meet the new demand in the suburbs; when they did agree to expansion, they often charged rates that the suburbs thought were excessive. Large numbers of suburbanites were forced to rely on septic tanks that caused widespread pollution of the water supply. In 1959 the State Department of Health reported that nearly half the individual home wells in thirty-nine suburban communities were polluted by residue from the backyard septic tanks. The Federal Housing Administration threatened to cease insuring mortgages for homes that were not tied into a central sewer system. This resulted in proposals for the creation of new independent sewer districts in the suburbs. But a proliferation of such districts would make the overall problem of controlling sewage treatment and disposal even more cumbersome than it already was. As an alternative, the MPC advocated a metropolitan sewage-disposal authority. The Legislature could not agree on any solution in its 1961, 1963, and 1965 sessions, however, and consensus was beginning to form around the idea of creating a new regional policy body that could define the area's comprehensive needs.

By 1965, the serious debate was not on whether there should be a regional agency, but on what kind of agency it should be. City-county consolidation was not seriously considered. In light of the failure of most consolidation schemes elsewhere,[10] the difficulty of merging five or more counties and at least two central cities seemed insurmountable. The reformers also feared a big, unresponsive super-government. Federation was rejected for similar reasons. Rather than needing a metropolitan-wide general-purpose government, reformers felt that the real need was for an agency that could *establish policy* for the metropolitan-wide governmental services such as transit, sewers, solid-waste disposal, water resources, air pollution, regional parks, and a metropolitan zoo. The reformers were especially concerned over the possibility that the staff of the Metropolitan Planning Commission would become the dominant actor in determining how federal grants would be awarded under the new metropolitan review powers established in 1966.[11]

Thus, the immediate motive force in 1966-67 for creating the Metropolitan Council was not predominantly grounded in theoretical concerns for metropolitan reform, as seems to have been the case in many other metropolises. Rather, the predominant motive was a practical concern for some immediate problems that could not be dealt with effectively under the existing governmental apparatus. On the sewage problem, the most influential reformers preferred creating a metropolitan-wide authority to creating several subregional agencies. But if a metropolitan sewer board were created, along with a metropolitan transit commission, and further down the track, more metropolitan agencies for parks, open space, and solid-waste disposal, there would be no comprehensive policy-making capacity at the metropolitan level. The general-purpose local governments would continue to lose influence to staff-dominated, single-purpose agencies, and it would be impossible to coordinate the developmental impacts of these various governments.

In fact, for the problem perceived by the Twin Cities reformers, no theoretical model existed. Consolidation models aimed to abolish local governments, but the Twin Cities reformers saw no need to do this. The two-tier models of Miami, Toronto, and London had some theoretical appeal, but the Twin Cities reformers were not seeking to create a general-purpose government at the metropolitan level, and in any case there did not seem to be any practical possibility of achieving such a drastic reorganization. What eventually emerged, in the view of Ted Kolderie, who was a key actor in the reform proceedings, was a metropolitan organization analogous to Alfred Sloan's model of organization at General Motors, with its centralized planning and its decentralized management of operations.[12] The concept was not clearly articulated in 1967, and, in fact, the reformers were deeply split over the question of whether the Metropolitan Council should be confined to policy making or whether it should also own and operate public facilities such as sewer, airport, and transit systems, But as the Council developed, the emerging desire was for one agency that would plan policies and an entirely different set of agencies that would deliver the public services. This dichotomy would require the political process to be more visible to the public and open to monitoring by the Legislature. A single agency that combined the planning and functional powers could both make and execute policy in private, and the reformers sought to avoid such a closed process.

A variety of specific institutional proposals were advanced by loose coalitions of municipal officials, the business and industrial community, the central-city newspapers, the governor, key state legislators, and leaders of both political parties. The Citizens League issued a report early in 1967 that appeared to crystallize many views into a workable plan.[13] It called for an elected Metropolitan Council that would have extensive policy-making and operating powers on sixteen metropolitan-wide problems. Opposition was socially and geographically scattered, limited mostly to county officials, some suburbs that were growing most rapidly, and a chain of suburban newspapers. Yet, the arguments of the opponents were blunted by the very real and continuing sewage-disposal problem. These opponents had organized late in the process and appeared to be too parochial to keep the Council from being created. As a consequence, most of the debate focused on the details of the Council's powers rather than on the question of whether or not a Metropolitan Council should be created.

All these forces for metropolitan reorganization came together in the 1967 session of the Legislature. The timing was propitious, since that was the first session after the 1966 Legislative reapportionment in compliance with the United States Supreme Court's *Reynolds v. Sims* one person-one vote decision. And metropolitan area representation was greatly increased. Minnesota's Legislature has traditionally been the preeminent political force in the state, and in the late 1960s it was dominated by strong leaders who were concerned about metropolitan reorganization. They believed that local leaders could not act on the issue, and they did not want to subject the question to a referendum. Although four distinct plans were laid before the lawmakers, a consensus steadily grew during four months of debate, and a bill finally emerged that changed the Metropolitan Planning Commission into the Metropolitan Council.

Not only was the Metropolitan Council distinct from a general-purpose government, it also differed significantly from the councils of government (COGs) that were being created in so many metropolises during the late 1960s to meet federal-government planning requirements. In the COGs, each county, central city, and large municipality is directly represented, and the financial contributions of these member governments are voluntary. In the Twin Cities, existing governments are *not* represented in the Metropolitan Council. Rather, by making the Council districts roughly coterminus with two State Senate districts, most of the Council districts cross over existing municipal and county boundaries. This makes it impossible for any given government in the metropolitan area to be directly represented on the Metropolitan Council. Also, rather than relying on voluntary contributions from existing governments, the Council was authorized a one-sixth mill property tax levy. These provisions gave the Twin Cities Metropolitan Council financial independence and made it impossible for the local governments to paralyze it as they have paralyzed so many of the COGs.[14]

The Metropolitan Council Appears

The creation of the Metropolitan Council was a political venture unlike any that has taken place before or since. Although it inherited the planning responsibilities of the MPC and continued to have a membership appointed by the governor with the consent of the Senate, it also embodied several innovations. First, in order to gain control over the maze of special districts, the new Council was given power to review their long-range comprehensive plans that had a substantial effect on metropolitan development. Special district plans that conflicted with the Council's *Metropolitan Development Guide* could be indefinitely suspended by the Council. Second, each municipality and township in the seven-county region was required to submit its comprehensive plans to the Council for review and comment on its implications for metropolitan development. The Council was not granted veto power over these, but it could negotiate in conflicts between any plan and either the *Metropolitan Development Guide* or a neighboring government's plan. Third, the Council was authorized to participate as a party in any proceedings before the Minnesota Municipal Commission concerning local-unit boundary changes. Although the rush of incorporation of very small communities had been ended earlier by the Municipal Commission, this role enabled the Council to make formal input into further decisions on annexations and incorporations. Finally, the Council was directed to appoint from its membership one person to serve on the Metropolitan Airports Commission, the Metropolitan Mosquito Control Commission, the Minneapolis-St. Paul Sanitary District (and it successor), and any other metropolitan commission to be established by the Legislature. These provisions forged a direct communication link for the Council to put its viewpoints before these other decision-making commissions.

It is significant to note that the Metropolitan Council is not, strictly speaking, a *local* government. Established by the state, and responsible to it alone, it was intended to fulfill the state's goals for its largest metropolitan area. Within its jurisdiction live nearly half of Minnesota's population (and legislators). The Legislature had long shown concern for the quality and efficiency of local government. By creating the Council it said, in effect, that a new tool was necessary to achieve efficient and quality government in this complex urban region. Yet, owing to its limited geographical scope, the Council is not fully a state agency. This undefined, intermediate position still stimulates questions over its "ultimate" status.

The creation of the Metropolitan Council is an example of a class of decisions that political scientists call *nonincremental*. Its opposite, the *incremental* decision process, consists of a series of relatively small changes made in a policy or budget over a period of time, none of them greatly innovative in itself. These steps are taken at such a pace that the impact of each can be evaluated before the next is taken, and the policy makers can minimize the mistakes resulting from untried changes. This chain of decisions can extend as far in time as necessary, with the flexibility to respond to new problems and opportunities as they appear.[15] By contrast, the nonincremental decision is a major innovative step taken at one time, committing new legal authority and/or large sums of money to a program that must start at a high level of effort if it is to have any chance of success.[16] The decision in the early 1960s to initiate the manned space program is one example of this, as were the choices of Atlanta and San Francisco to build rapid transit systems. The establishment of a new government agency with powers that had never been exercised before would also be a nonincremental decision.

Although the Metropolitan Council was built on several precedents set by the Metropolitan Planning Commission, its new relationships to the special districts and local governments were so innovative as not to be identifiable as simple increments. Those relationships had to be established if the Council was to make any progress at all on the sanitation and urban-sprawl problems. The act was a major "calculated risk" for the state and local decision makers. Like any nonincremental decision, it has a higher potential for accomplishment, but this is matched by a greater potential for failure and uncertainty of outcome. Only time would tell whether the new Council would turn out to be simply a rubber stamp for the special districts or whether it would agressively invade the cherished perogatives of the local governments.

Incremental Evolution
of the Metropolitan Council

Creating the Council was a nonincremental decision, but keeping it in operation to achieve the legislators' objectives would require many further decisions—many incremental adjustments, in other words. The metropolitan organizations established in Miami, Jacksonville, and Nashville can be altered only by charter amendments approved by popular vote, a cumbersome and uncertain process. But what the Minnesota Legislature established, it could change. So the Metropolitan Council and the entire metropolitan governance structure is much better suited to incremental development. Consisting as it does of separate planning and functional agencies, it is relatively easy to expand, restructure, and change priorities for.

The 1969 Increments

When the Legislature created the Council in 1967, it also charged the Council with developing proposals for coping with a series of metropolitan problems including water pollution, solid-waste disposal, and regional parks, among other subjects. The Council responded with specific legislative proposals for the 1969 session. Its major proposal was to deal with the sewer problems by creating the Metropolitan Sewer Board. The Sewer Board would own and operate the region's sewer system, but the Council would appoint the Board's members and would prepare a long-range plan for the Board to implement. The Legislature adopted this recommendation and in so doing solidified the basic metropolitan governance model that has remained the same ever since. Overall policy making is vested in the Metropolitan Council, and operations and day-to-day program implementation are carried out by the functional agencies.

In addition to adopting the Council's recommendations on the sewer question, the Legislature established lines of coordination between the Council and the Metropolitan Transit Commission which had been established independently of the Council in 1967. The Council also received increased planning authority in the areas of open-space protection, airport development, solid waste, and highways.

These legislative actions in 1969 established a pattern that served as a precedent for Legislature-Council relations in future years. First, the Legislature gave priority consideration to the Council's policy proposals. Second, although granting specific responsibilities to the Council, the Legislature made clear that it intended to review the Council's performances after a biennium and to make any needed adjustments. Each decision increment was thus based on some evaluation of how previous decisions had been carried out.

The 1971 Increments

The 1971 legislative session saw moves to "fine tune" the new system of metropolitan governance. Policy differences were beginning to emerge between the Council and the Metropolitan Transit Commission (MTC). The Legislature ordered the MTC to implement the transit elements of the Council's transportation development program. Watershed districts were placed under the Council's planning controls, and the counties' development plans were subjected to the same review and comment procedure as was used with the municipalities. Meanwhile, the Council continued to work on its *Development Guide*, and by 1971 had completed chapters on six functions. Yet, comprehensive planning was slow, owing to time and money constraints and the pressures to resolve the more concrete and immediate problems.

The 1973-74 Increments

By the opening of the 1973 legislative session, it became apparent that further decisions were needed in the areas of parks, housing, and transit. The role of the Metropolitan Council itself also needed to be clarified. It was not clear how much authority each metropolitan agency had to make plans and set priorities for capital expenditures. This problem was most acute in the public-transit sector. Late in 1972, the MTC revealed its plan for a fifty-seven-mile, rail, rapid-transit system to cost 1 billion dollars on completion in 1990. This conflicted with an earlier Council policy statement which called for a transportation system that relied on expanded bus and small-vehicle service. Although the MTC recognized the discrepancy, it claimed a statutory charge to forward its own plan to the Legislature. It did so and requested funding for it. The lawmakers thus faced not only the choice of a transit system, but also the issue of deciding which agency had final authority over such planning.

The Metropolitan Council proposed some major changes in its own structure as well as in its relationship to other metropolitan agencies. Because reapportionment had increased the number of Senate districts in the seven-county region, the Council's membership had to be increased in order to retain the principle of one Metropolitan Council district for every two Senate districts. The Council favored that increase and urged that the members be elected from districts for six-year terms (except the chairperson, who would remain a governor's appointee). It also recommended that the Council appoint the chairperson of the Sewer Board and future members of the MTC and MAC (which were then made up of local officials or their appointees and a chairperson selected by the governor). Additionally, the Council requested authority to sell bonds to finance county purchase of parklands as well as the power to serve as a regional housing authority.

The Legislature was not ready to digest so many metropolitan issues in that session. The House approved the MTC's transit plan, but the Senate's Metropolitan and Urban Affairs Committee refused to endorse either plan. Instead, it concentrated on the jurisdictional question. The Committee believed that only the Metropolitan Council could have a broad enough perspective to assess the costs, benefits, and land-use impact of transportation planning. Thus, the committee drafted a long, complex bill that strengthened the Council's policy-making role and provided for the election of Council members. The full Senate, however, refused to accept such a drastic change. The bill got caught up in the end-of-session rush, and the entire matter was put off until the following year. Owing to a constitutional amendment, 1974 was to be the first regular legislative session in an even-numbered year.

During the intervening year, support developed for the changes, and the Metropolitan Reorganization Act passed in 1974. This act increased the Council's membership to seventeen (but kept it appointed), gave the Council power to appoint MTC members (but not the chairperson), power to approve the development programs of the MTC and the Waste Control Commission (the former Sewer Board), and power to approve the capital expenditures of the Metropolitan Airports Commission (MAC).

The Reorganization Act also gave the Council power to review the metropolitan significance of public and private projects, once the Council had adopted standards for determining metropolitan significance and the Legislature had approved them. This was an unprecedented power to give to a metropolitan agency. It meant that no housing project could be built, no shopping center constructed, no development whatsoever could be undertaken if the Council determined it to be of metropolitan significance and contrary to the Council's development plans. The Council's request for park bonding and housing powers was also granted. In the transit debate, the Council's authority was upheld, as both houses concurred that the MTC's proposal was unsuited to such a decentralized region as the Twin Cities. Instead, the Legislature increased appropriations for bus improvements and operations.

The 1975-76 Increments

Early in 1975 the Council adopted a Development Framework which called for dividing the region between an urban-service and a rural-service area. The urban-service area was scheduled for substantial investment in sewers and highways to accommodate future growth. The rural-service area was scheduled for very limited public services to keep the population at a low density. By restricting development to areas already equipped to accommodate it, rather than permitting sprawl to continue at the current rate, the Council estimated that up to 2 billion dollars in public investments could be saved over the next fifteen years. However, if this growth limitation were to be enforced, the Council would need a power it did not then have—to prohibit cities and counties from planning or approving urban development in the rural-service area. To secure this further increment, the Council asked the Legislature for the land-use planning powers necessary to implement its Development Framework.

This was to be the largest single increment in the ten-year development of the Metropolitan Council, and it generated considerable opposition. Many local officials and many representatives of the housing-construction industry resisted giving the Council power actually to prevent development in certain areas. Their arguments led the Senate to defeat the bill by two votes in 1975. One observer noted that proposed governmental structure changes are often voted down at least once before passage in a later session.

Forcing metropolitan and local levels of government to talk to one another, to plan in concert with one another, evidently implied so major a change that it would take longer to accomplish. But even the Republican Minority Leader in the Senate stated publicly he believed the bill would pass in the next session.[17]

Passage did come in 1976 after some House-Senate compromises on the bill. According to the terms of the Metropolitan Land Planning Act of 1976, the Metropolitan Council was required to prepare a systems statement for each municipality and county of the seven-county region by July 1, 1977. That statement was to show precisely how the metropolitan systems plans of sewers, parks, transit, and airports would affect each municipality and county in the region. Each of these local governments then has three years, until July 1, 1980, to prepare a comprehensive development plan and submit it to the Council for review. The local plans must be consistent with the metropolitan systems plans. If not, the local governments may be told to modify any part that substantially departs from that statement. In the legislative debates, the local governments were especially concerned over the way in which differences in judgment between the Metropolitan Council and a city or county would be resolved. Essentially, the Council will decide, after a public hearing, although the local government may appeal to the courts.

Because the Land Planning Act would require local governments to spend money developing their plans, the Council is also empowered to make grants to assist local units in preparing their plans or to prepare plans for the local governments if they request. As a final effort to calm local fears, the law also provides for a Council-appointed committee, at least half of which is to consist of elected local officials, to advise the Council on the use of its land-control powers. A late amendment to the bill ordered the Council to prepare a plan for expanding the supply of modest-cost housing on vacant residential land. Although the Council had already been pressing the suburbs to make such provisions, this increment endorsed that policy and laid the foundation for a stronger legislative mandate.

The 1977 Increments

The Council did not propose to the lawmakers at the beginning of 1977 any changes in its structure or major new responsibilities. It did ask for, and received, additional money for regional parks acquisition, its highest-priority item, plus additional sums for park trails. The Legislature also mandated all counties in the metropolitan area to establish the "911" emergency telephone service by 1982 and required the Council to establish the system's design standards. Since the Council had been planning this for several years, the law, in effect, endorsed its work. Other acts expanded the Council's responsibilities in transit and criminal-justice planning. Finally, it was given an ambiguous role in planning for a new metropolitan sports stadium; the questions surrounding this are analyzed in Chapter 6.

There were also bills before the lawmakers to require the popular election of Council members, although varying in the procedures. However, in the continued absence of consensus on the issue and on the manner and timing of the voting, the bills were held in committee for further study. The Legislature did not act on the problem of housing costs, awaiting more specific Council proposals than were contained in the report of the Modest-Cost Housing Advisory Committee.

Conclusion

When all the increments have been added, what emerges is a metropolitan governing structure that has far transcended the one which first appeared in 1967. The innovation that was collectively embodied in the successive increments equals in impact, if it does not surpass, that first nonincremental step. Yet, the evidence supports Ted Kolderie's assertion that over the years the Legislature "has maintained the concept of a coordinating council required to focus its energies on policy considerations and forced to give direction to implementing agencies at all levels."[18]

It is important also that the Metropolitan Council is not just a planning and coordinating agency, albeit an authoritative one. The Legislature also created a political decision-making structure, manned by persons with considerable political as well as planning skills. The Council has come to function as an arena within which many controversies and choices of regional importance can be discussed, negotiated, and even settled to the extent possible. As Edward Knudson indicates, the ideas of the planners did not merely remain in the realm of "big concepts" or "technical solutions," but they came to make up the agenda for debate within a system that had power to make real decisions.[19] Such a political agency could not have sprung full-grown out of a single legislative session, nor could its evolution have been plotted with precision ten years in advance. Only an incremental process, building on the initial threshold-crossing decision and the sense of direction prevailing in a strong legislative body, could have produced the metropolitan governing structure as it is today. The nature of this governing structure will be outlined in the next chapter.

CHAPTER 3

The Metropolitan Council Today

Despite the many incremental changes made by the Legislature over
ten years, the Metropolitan Council remains what it was intended
to be: a planning and policy-making agency for guiding the physical
and social development of the region and delivering regional public
services. It does not directly provide services or control land use.
The impact that its actions have is conveyed by the other 272 units
of local government in the region, whose existence has not been
affected by the Council's emergence (except for the metropolitan
agencies, to be described later). Yet, in matters of defined metropolitan impact, the Council can either prevent or compel actions
by these other units, and it has a broad though noncoercive sphere
of influence beyond that. It also exerts some influence over state
agency actions in the metropolitan area, such as the Department
of Transportation's highway planning.

Jurisdiction and Organization
of the Metropolitan Council

The Metropolitan Council exercises jurisdiction over the seven
counties of Anoka, Carver, Dakota, Hennepin, Ramsey, Scott, and
Washington. As shown in Figure 3.1, this includes the cities of Minneapolis and St. Paul, their suburban ring, and a rural fringe in

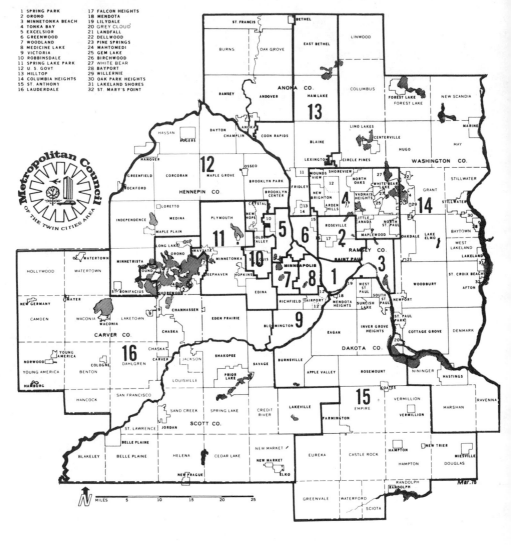

METROPOLITAN COUNCIL OF THE TWIN CITIES AREA

The Council members and their districts are as follows: Chairman - John Boland, North St. Paul

1 - John J. Costello,
    St. Paul
2 - Todd J. Lefko,
    St. Paul
3 - Charles L. Rafferty,
    St. Paul
4 - Stanley B. Kegler,
    Maplewood

5 - George Dahlvang,
    Minneapolis
6 - Joan Campbell,
    Minneapolis
7 - Gladys S. Brooks,
    Minneapolis
8 - Alton J. Gasper,
    Minneapolis

9 - Patrick W. Colbert, Jr.,
    Bloomington
10 - Betty Kane,
    Golden Valley
11 - Robert Short,
    Edina
12 - Charles R. Weaver,
    Anoka

13 - Marcia Bennett,
    Columbia Heights
14 - Opal M. Petersen,
    Stillwater
15 - Gary Pagel,
    West St. Paul
16 - M. James Daly,
    Belle Plaine

Figure 3-1. Metropolitan Council districts. Courtesy of the Metropolitan Council.

which some urbanization has taken place. The region's population is 1,973,000, according to the Council's 1977 estimate. The Standard Metropolitan Statistical Area is actually larger than this, encompassing three counties that are now experiencing growth pressures, but for which the Council has no authority to plan. Any expansion of the Council's geographic jurisdiction is very unlikely, owing to strong opposition from the areas that would be included.

It would be misleading to think of the Metropolitan Council as a single monolithic entity. A more realistic image is that of four components, which are all the "Council" but have different personnel and roles. The first is the literal Council—the seventeen members appointed by the governor of Minnesota and confirmed by the Senate. This is the final decision-making authority. Then there is the Council as represented by its chairman, a full-time person who both presides over Council meetings and (at present) directs its staff. Third, there is the Council's staff, which performs the ongoing research, planning, and other duties. Finally, the Council organization encompasses the citizen advisory committees, which make major inputs into the decision-making process. Each of these components is discussed in turn.

The Council itself consists of seventeen members. Sixteen represent districts with an average population of 125,000 each and serve four-year terms. Half the terms expire every two years. Members receive $50 per diem for attending each of the twice monthly meetings and for other meetings that are officially authorized. They have represented a variety of occupational backgrounds, but can generally be characterized as "civic leaders" in their communities or in the region as a whole. No local government officials serve on it. Although the post is officially nonpartisan, most appointments have reflected the party affiliation of the governor who made them. In 1977, seven of the eight incumbents were reappointed, continuing a trend toward low turnover, a combined choice of the governor and the incumbents themselves.

The seventeenth member of the Council is the chairperson, whom the law prescribes be "experienced in the field of municipal and urban affairs with administrative training and executive ability."[1] The first chairman was James Hetland, a law professor at the University of Minnesota, who served from 1967 to 1971. When Wendell

Anderson took office as governor in 1971, he replaced Hetland with Minneapolis alderman Albert Hofstede, who held the post for two years and resigned to run successfully for mayor of that city. The current chairman is John Boland, a former high-school teacher and two-term state representative before Anderson selected him in 1973. The chairman presides over Council meetings and has one vote, but no veto power. The Council's by-laws designate him chief executive, with power to prepare and submit the annual budget and create Council committees. His salary is set by the Legislature and currently is $39,000 per year.

The three chairmen present a sharp contrast in leadership roles. Hetland saw the Council as a distinctly *metropolitan* agency whose chief constituency was the Legislature. Thus, he sought to lead the members in extended debate of regional policy issues and to make decisions that were its alone and not endorsements of a consensus achieved elsewhere. To do its job, the Council had to say no to local units on occasion in defense of regional interests. Hetland saw himself as a member of the Council, distinct from the staff and its daily operations. He related with that staff through an executive director. For him the post was part-time as he continued teaching law.

Hetland's successor, Albert Hofstede, saw the chairman's job as a full-time position. He also saw the Council as entering a new phase in its existence. Hetland had successfully guided the Council through its transition from a planning agency to a policy-making body, and under his leadership the Council had acquired considerable political legitimacy, particularly from its successful recommendations for handling the sewer crisis. On a number of other issues, however, the Council had not gotten beyond the plan-making stage. As a result, Hofstede perceived one of the major tasks of his chairmanship to be that of translating the plans into actual policy decisions. Many of the original *Development Guide* chapters were adopted during this period, and action was begun on other chapters which were not actually adopted until later. As the Council began drafting and adopting these policy chapters, it came into sharp conflict with other political actors in the metropolis. Its airport chapter left open the prospect of reserving a northern site for a second airport. Its transportation chapter brough the Council into conflict with the Metropolitan Transit Commission over that agency's plan to build a rapid-transit system. And its decision during this period to oblige the suburbs to plan for some subsidized low-income housing brought the Council into direct conflict with a number of suburban municipalities. These conflicts were just beginning to come to a head when Hofstede resigned as chairman to run for mayor of Minneapolis.

His successor, John Boland, entered office with the perception that the Metropolitan Council was under growing attack by the city and county officials as a result of its policies and its manner of dealing with them. He expected that if this opposition continued to grow, it could undermine its support in the Legislature. Thus, he defined those local officials as the Council's chief constituency, and he concentrated on repairing relationships with them. This involved attending many local meetings and appointing a Chairman's Advisory Committee made up of the more concerned municipal leaders. This committee became a forum for sharing problems and ideas. Boland's chairmanship has been characterized by an openness to bargain and compromise on policy issues. This enabled him to win many local officials' support for the 1976 Metropolitan Land Planning Act, after the bill had been revised to meet their most serious objections. Like Hofstede, Boland made his post full-time, but went further by releasing the executive director and assuming his duties. He thus bridges the gap between Council and staff and has put much pressure on the latter to support his conciliatory style of dealing with the local governments.

In several respects, the three chairman worked in similar ways. All have given much time to speaking engagements to educate the public on the Council. Equally important, they have worked closely with the Legislature to build and hold their political support. As a result, the Council has had a remarkably successful record of getting its high-priority bills passed by the Legislature. Clearly, the chairmen have been key actors in the incremental process of expanding their own agency's responsibilities.

Much of the Council's decision making takes place in its three committees, as indicated in the organization chart in Figure 3-2. The committee members are appointed by the Council chairman and normally meet weekly. The Personnel and Work Program Committee makes recommendations to the full Council on internal management, the budget, the yearly work program, and proposals

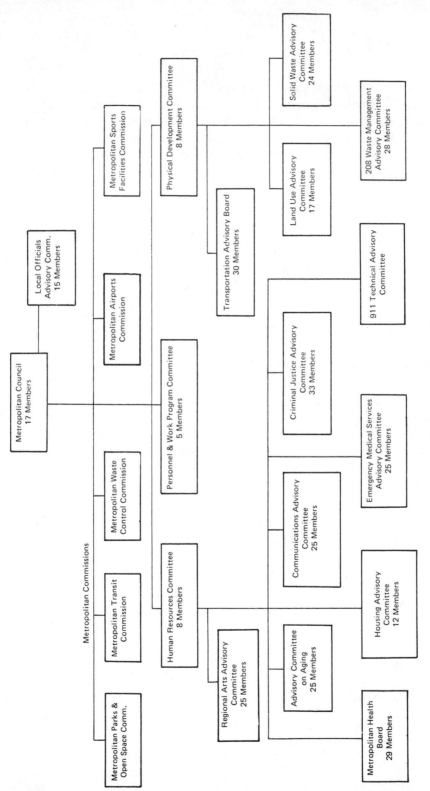

Figure 3-2. Metropolitan Council policy-making structure. Courtesy of the Metropolitan Council.

to the Legislature. The Human Resources Committee is responsible for the *Development Guide* chapters on social policies and preparation of the Social Framework, and makes preliminary decisions on local grant applications for federal and state funds within those policy areas. Finally, the Physical Development Committee is concerned with the physical systems and land-use chapters of the *Guide* and the overall Development Framework. It monitors the local planning efforts and reviews the grant requests relevant to those functions. Generally, the full Council readily approves committee proposals and actions.

The staff consisted of 174 persons, as of February 1977. As shown in Figure 3-3, it is organized into four departments. The bulk of the professional staff members have education and experience in various aspects of social and physical planning. The budget for the staff support totaled $5,270,000 in 1977, with the largest single items of expenditure in the categories of environmental and transportation planning. Tables 3-1 and 3-2 indicate the sources of the Council's revenue and its expenditures in 1977, categorized by object of expenditure and by function. The federal and state grants that are received are earmarked for specific planning projects. The property tax funds are derived from an 8/30 mill levy, a rate set by the Legislature.

Citizens may participate in Metropolitan Council decision making through a set of policy boards and advisory committees, as well as the public hearings that must precede the final adoption of major policy statements. At the beginning of 1977, there were 563 members in eleven such committees and their subcommittees (see Figure 3-2).[2] As the Council moves into new areas, new advisory committees are formed. In 1977, for example, an Emergency Medical Services Advisory Committee was established, with twenty-five members. The committees hold regular public meetings to study and make recommendations on their assignments and invite interested parties to testify. Some committees, such as those on aging and criminal justice, screen applications for federal and state grants for projects in their policy areas and rank them in order of merit in their reports to the Council. The Metropolitan Housing and Redevelopment Authority Advisory Committee actively supervises housing programs for suburban communities that request its services. Be-

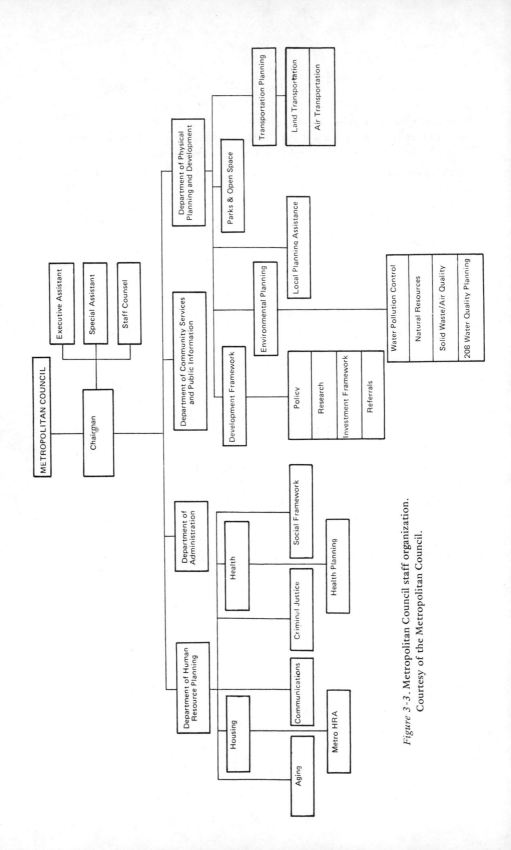

Figure 3-3. Metropolitan Council staff organization. Courtesy of the Metropolitan Council.

Table 3-1. Metropolitan Council Statement of Revenue and Expenditures for All
Planning Funds, 1977 (October, November, and December Estimated)

Revenue

Real and Personal Property Taxes

Anoka County	$ 137,901.96
Carver County	25,705.06
Dakota County	165,666.18
Hennepin County	953,665.50
Ramsey County	382,120.84
Scott County	31,893.72
Washington County	85,712.22
State of Minnesota: Homestead Credit	370,903.93
State of Minnesota: Local Aide	79,152.04
State of Minnesota: Agricultural Aide	6,512.36
Total Taxes	$2,239,233.81

Regional Commissions

Metropolitan Airports Commission	$ 92,192.00
Metropolitan Transit Commission	183,761.00
Metropolitan Waste Control Commission	424,723.00
Total Commission Reimbursement	700,676.00
Federal, State, and Local Grants	2,505,476.71
Interest Earned on Investments	27,866.87
Fund Balance	(200,000.00)
Total Revenue	$5,273,253.19

Expenditures: Direct and Indirect

Salaries and Benefits	$3,809,437.46
Travel, Registration, and Conference Fees	12,122.37
Travel, Local	10,791.46
Travel, Nonlocal	44,605.15
Recruitment	15,439.08
Employee Development	3,501.47
Membership Dues	15,241.70
Communications: Telephone	65,794.82
Communications: Postage	89,500.93
Communications: Legal Notices and Public Hearings	21,563.77
Reproduction and Publication	205,321.06
Library Services	13,699.27
Office Rent and Utilities	259,782.05
Members Expense	118,976.11
Communications: Wats	7,428.95
Insurance and Bonds	18,299.57
Rent of Equipment	(705.86)
Office Supplies	14,551.56
Maintenance of Equipment	10,440.55
User Charge	48,853.54
Accounting Service	10,932.54
Computer Service	110,510.25
Miscellaneous Expenses	18,637.86
Interest on Certificates	20,397.50
Legal Service	20,784.30
Consultants	244,411.77
Contractual Services with Others	62,933.96
Total Expenditures	$5,273,253.19

47

Table 3-2. Metropolitan Council Major Federal Planning Project Funds Statement
of Cumulative Revenue and Expenditures as of December 31, 1977
(October, November, and December Estimated)

REVENUE AND EXPENDITURES	Aging	Census Preparation	Criminal Justice
Revenue			
Direct Federal Grants	$	$120,081.99	$
Contributions from Local Agencies	164,945.00		211,068.00
Agency Contributions	37,896.86	40,027.33	66,544.44
Total Revenue	$202,841.86	$160.109.31	$277,612.44
Expenditures: Direct and Indirect			
Salaries and Benefits	$157,756.33	$127,713.34	$217,319.45
Travel, Registration, and Conference Fees	604.75	295.27	588.40
Travel, Local	254.43	1,563.87	1,560.66
Travel, Nonlocal	1,895.33	693.10	4,177.72
Recruitment	543.11	466.79	1,232.66
Employee Development	73.19	110.26	98.83
Membership Dues	1.48	2.21	1.88
Communications: Telephone	3,077.92	1,747.90	3,620.37
Communications: Postage	4,109.87	3,562.98	3,994.40
Communications: Legal Notices and Public Hearings	210.65	338.08	351.95
Reproduction and Publication	11,961.92	3,858.00	10,010.42
Library Services	600.17	810.24	743.88
Office Rent and Utilities	11,023.93	8,360.14	13,834.12
Members Expense	1,747.56	64.41	1,750.18
Communications: Wats	256.85	235.55	522.45
Insurance and Bonds	346.32	282.57	398.25
Rent of Equipment	142.92	(41.18)	(77.93)
Office Supplies	369.47	324.61	648.94
Maintenance of Equipment	533.95	566.43	498.90
User Charge	2,565.52	1,786.61	2,876.83
Accounting Service	403.95	653.59	491.42
Computer Service	2,117,77	4,192.23	2,942.03
Miscellaneous Expenses	109.83	228.70	134.53
Legal Service	236.85	341.08	306.39
Consultants	651.08	1,106.87	5,818.69
Contractual Services with Others	1,246.71	845.86	3,737.02
Total Expenditures	$202,841.86	$160,109.31	$177,612.44

Table 3-2 — Continued

Health	HUD 701	Land Transportation	Social Framework	Water Quality 201	Water Quality 208
$629,371.89	$388,000.00	$239,450.00	$ 84,130.00	$	$261,893.77
42,200.00		340,617.00		241,784.83	
42,200.00	212,455.46	115,079.59	101,269.55	9,631.89	87,297.92
$713,771.89	$600,455.46	$695,146.59	$185,399.55	$251,416.72	$349,191.69
$462,052.57	$473,577.36	$482,625.04	$154,723.32	$213,926.31	$233,929.63
2,124.93	1,838.48	830.23	561.53	370.56	1,215.37
714.26	1,260.56	1,134.68	168.73	1,201.75	443.73
4,383.99	3,540.05	9,351.93	1,284.88	1,620.59	4,724.69
3,426.64	351.68	1,747.49	897.92	33.39	524.67
301.24	1,155.08	191.77	782.83	93.08	97.35
1,619.99	4.37	3.33	.91	2.04	1.37
8,061.86	8,973.11	7,009.28	2,529.83	1,751.19	2,165.75
17,439.68	9,532.31	8,083.96	2,211.41	4,107.95	3,808.64
9,747.89	1,079.00	709.28	217.24	276.79	841.85
45,467.99	33,157.52	15,923.77	4,040.99	7,219.46	6,669.68
1,774.60	1,680.96	1,561.67	510.56	773.71	706.52
31,964.10	33,942.13	32,212.43	7,738.77	9,123.07	9,820.23
9,501.70	1,152.20	1,132.08	635.51	66.19	456.33
880.59	1,154.07	1,573.96	207.74	202.90	409.23
578.05	910.57	919.32	213.80	422.45	395.21
38.47	56.17	(110.19)	26.56	(105.24)	(80.47)
2,599.09	1,079.52	2,675.80	244.15	583.50	569.08
973.12	1,322.87	1,348.31	331.83	597.36	471.37
5,510.86	6,105.64	6,547.92	1,903.44	2,556.53	2,383.00
1,570.44	1,137.04	1,014.72	466.13	501.85	500.81
25,111.07	8,903.05	34,312.51	1,822.91	3,344.10	2,514.87
295.39	319.24	299.72	92.61	142.30	193.71
896.69	911.92	610.56	250.75	298.02	302.00
63,574.06	2,805.57	76,681.33	773.20	902.21	68,925.95
11,162.62	4,504.99	6,755.69	2,762.00	1,404.63	7,201.12
$713,771.89	$600,455.46	$695,146.59	$185,399.55	$251,416.72	$349,191.69

sides these permanent committees, temporary advisory committees and task forces are created from time to time.

The Council appoints most of the members of these committees, but some selections are made by local government officials and other organizations. Some appointees must meet certain criteria, such as professional experience in the committee's subject. To broaden the pool of potential members, the Council in 1976 began to advertise all vacancies publicly and invite applications from interested persons. By the end of that year, this "open appointments" process had produced more than 2,000 applicants. In 1977, a special task force was created to study the appointment process and make recommendations on improving it.

Generally, there is on each committee a combination of disinterested citizens and representatives of the various interest groups affected. A glance at some of their membership lists, however, suggests that the latter tend to outweigh the former. In 1976, for example, the Transportation Advisory Board, which assists in preparing an overall transportation policy plan, included seven suburban municipal officials, seven county commissioners, a council member from each of the two central cities, the chairman of the Metropolitan Transit Commission, the commissioner of the Minnesota Department of Transportation, at least one trucking-firm owner, and a representative of the Minnesota Pollution Control Agency. Twenty-one of its thirty members are appointed by entities other than the Council, formally structuring this special-interest representation into the Board. Generally, this method of securing citizen participation is a means for getting interested parties to explore compromises on sensitive issues before the Council must make a final decision. But it may also serve to shield that body from pressures to experiment with new approaches or proposals not endorsed by the interests represented on the advisory committees.

Generally, the public hearings have not led to substantial changes in the texts of proposed *Development Guide* chapters. This suggests that the hearings may be more a legal formality than a channel for citizen preferences into the policy process. Indeed, they may simply enable the Council to increase public awareness of, and support for, its policy proposals. Much of this is speculation, however, because no systematic study has yet been done on this issue.

For all the stress on citizen participation, the Metropolitan Council remains closely tied to the Minnesota Legislature for its authority and major policy directions, as the developmental process has continually reaffirmed. It must present annual reports to the lawmakers and is expected to draft legislative proposals for each session. In turn, the Legislature has used the Council as its research and advisory arm on numerous metropolitan issues. Its closest relationships are to the House Local and Urban Affairs Committee and the Senate Government Operations Committee, to which are referred nearly all bills with a metropolitan orientation. In a sense, also, all the legislators whose districts are in the seven-county region are the Council's "constituents." By contrast, Governors Levander, Anderson, and Perpich have played minimal roles in Council affairs apart from the appointment process and being generally supportive. The Council maintains close relationships with such state administrative units as the State Planning Agency, Pollution Control Agency, Housing Finance Agency, and Department of Transportation.

As a complement to its responsibilities to the state government, the Metropolitan Council also acts in many ways as an instrument of national urban policy. Essentially, it is one of those institutions for metropolitan policy making that Congress and the federal agencies sought to establish after 1965. Although it would probably still exist if those efforts had not been made, it would undoubtedly have less power today. This national urban policy has two faces, however. In one sense, it contains substantive goals that have been set by Congress for all metropolitan areas to meet in one way or another — an improved physical environment or broader housing opportunities for low-income persons. But the other face calls on metropolitan areas to define their own distinctive goals for growth and services. They must become capable of self-government as whole regions, able to choose within the broad (and sometimes nonexistent) guidelines of federal policy. The Council's organization and operations must be understood in light of both aspects, and this attempt to serve the possibly contradictory functions inevitably leads it into difficulties.

As a consequence, the Council functions as a gateway for a wide variety of project grant applications, a conduit for the federal and state funds that flow to the metropolitan area, and an advocate for the region in federal policy and program decision making.

In one respect, however, the Council does not fit Congress's "ideal model" of a metropolitan coordinating body. The legislation that requires the review process envisions a council made up largely or entirely of local elected officials—the standard way of constituting a regional council of governments or planning commission. It has been necessary for Minnesota's congressional delegation to secure amendments to each law permitting the review to be performed by a body established by a state legislature for that purpose; this makes the Metropolitan Council eligible to participate. This legal maneuvering raises the larger question of which level of government—national or state—should finally decide how metropolitan institutions should be structured.

Responsibilities and Powers
of the Metropolitan Council

The Metropolitan Council has a matrix of responsibilities that constitutes its pivotal role between the federal and state governments, on the one hand, and the local and regional authorities, on the other. These cover the spectrum from research and exploratory planning to the powers necessary to implement certain of its plans. Its functions encompass all the public policy issues that the Legislature has, in successive increments, defined as of regional importance, but the extent of its authority varies widely from one issue to another. For the purposes of this discussion, these responsibilities can be categorized in seven groups.

Preparing the Metropolitan Development Guide

First, the Council is charged with preparing a comprehensive *Development Guide* for the region. As described in the statutes, this guide

shall consist of a compilation of policy statements, goals, standard programs, and maps prescribing guides for an orderly and economic development, public and private, of the metropolitan area. The comprehensive development guide shall recognize and encompass physical, social or economic needs of the metropolitan area and those future developments which will have an impact on the entire area including but not limited to such matters as land use, parks and open space land needs, the necessity for and location of airports, highways, transit facilities, public hospitals, libraries, schools, and other public buildings.[3]

This guide is not a once-for-all-time master plan, as are many "metropolitan plans," whose finality has robbed them of any continuing influence. Rather, it is a set of policy statements emerging from a continuous and systematic planning process that enables the policies to be updated as new conditions and opportunities appear. The guide consists of thirteen chapters on functional topics such as waste management, transportation, health, housing, law and justice, and recreation. Its keystone is the Development Framework chapter, adopted in 1975 to provide some common goals and organizing principles for the functional statements and to define land-use policies on the urbanizing fringe of the region. Each of these is discussed separately in Chapter 4 or 5.

Over the years, this planning process has enlarged the first responsibility into that of being an arena for regional policy making. One observer has stated:

The Metropolitan Council views its responsibility first and foremost as the formulation of regional policy, one aspect of which is to collect the specific actions of both state and local levels of government and to make recommendations, mainly in the form of policy statements, to both the state and local municipalities for future laws and ordinances.[4]

As a consequence, a type of "regional politician" has emerged, whose interests and efforts are shaped and defined by the development framework process. These individuals are found not only in the Council and its staff, but also in the Legislature, in local governments and agencies, and in private business and civic organizations. Although growth management and public-service policies often lack public visibility and attention in the complex metropolitan public sector, they are clearly essential to its functioning.

Reviewing Local Government Plans

The Metropolitan Council's second responsibility is to review the comprehensive plans of all cities, townships, and counties in the region that have such plans—among the counties, Hennepin and Ramsey lack these planning powers. At present, it can only comment on the compatibility of those plans with the *Development Guide* and advise changes when it finds a conflict. As a result of the 1976 Metropolitan Land Planning Act, however, it will be able to require each local unit by 1980 to prepare and submit to it a comprehensive plan. This plan must address existing and future land uses, protection of the environment, housing opportunities, and the provision of public facilities such as transportation, sewers, and parks. Counties are to make similar plans for their unincorporated areas and also to locate solid-waste disposal sites. Before submitting the plans to the Council, each unit must also send a copy to all adjacent and overlapping governmental units, including school districts, for review and comment. When the Council examines the plans, it will consider their compatibility with each other as well as their consistency with the various chapters of the *Development Guide*. If it finds that some plan, in part or whole, conflicts substantially with its stated metropolitan system policies for sewers, transportation, airports, or recreational open space, it can require a change to bring it into conformity. School districts must also submit their programs for major capital improvements, but the Council is limited to making nonbinding recommendations on them. Figure 3-4 outlines the timetable that will be followed in this planning and review process.

It is the intent of the law to avoid "bitter end" confrontation between the Council and local officials, and so it provides for multi-stage communications during the review process to give many opportunities for coming to agreement. However, if a local unit does not want to make a mandated change, it can request a hearing of its case. The hearing will be conducted either by the Council's Land Use Advisory Committee or by a state hearing examiner, and after the hearing the case will be reconsidered by the Council. If the local unit does not accept that outcome, it can appeal to the state courts.

The intended outcomes of this augmentation of the Council's powers are clear. There will now be a process by which it can interact regularly with the local governments while retaining the final authority to set policy on matters of region-wide concern. If it came to a power struggle over such matters, the Council would triumph (subject always to long-range checks by the Legislature and the courts). But two other results were also anticipated by the lawmakers. Local units must now do comprehensive planning for their own futures, no longer leaving their development to discrete, ad hoc decisions. As of 1976, 44 percent of the metropolitan communities had never adopted any comprehensive plan.[5] Ideally, an effective planning process can enable a city or county to assert its own values and goals more clearly in the metropolitan political arena. Finally, since local plans must be referred to adjacent and overlapping governments, many interlocal conflicts should be resolved without Council intervention.

As the first stage in implementing these mandatory review powers, the Council conducted thirty meetings in 1976 with local officials to discuss the requirements of the Land Planning Act. Council staff held over 400 meetings with local officials in 1977. The Council is consulting with a seventeen-member Land Use Advisory Committee, made up of both local officials and private citizens, required by that law to provide input to the policy and administrative decisions. The Council also distributed more than a million dollars in planning funds that the Legislature had appropriated to help the local governments conduct the planning. In 1977, it submitted to each locality its systems statement for the four metropolitan systems—sewers, transportation, airports, and regional parks.

Coordinating Metropolitan Commissions and Special Districts

The Metropolitan Council oversees and coordinates the metropolitan commissions and special districts. The Twin Cities approach to this task is unique among metropolitan areas. Special districts have a strong propensity to operate independently of other units of local government. And, unless held in check by strong legal and policy tools, they often tend to conflict with them or with each other when their basic interests are at stake. The most common means of combating this excessive autonomy is having the districts' governing boards composed of officials of the constituent local units or their appointees. Ideally, these persons ensure that the districts cooperate effectively with the general-purpose governments. Another approach is to give several major functions to one special district, along with the responsibility to maintain their compatibility. Neither of these devices has proved very satisfactory in other metropolises.[6]

In the Twin Cities region, two different kinds of metropolitan districts exist. First, there are three *metropolitan commissions*—

Figure 3-4.

Planning Process for Counties, Municipalities, Townships, and School Districts.

Courtesy of the Metropolitan Council.

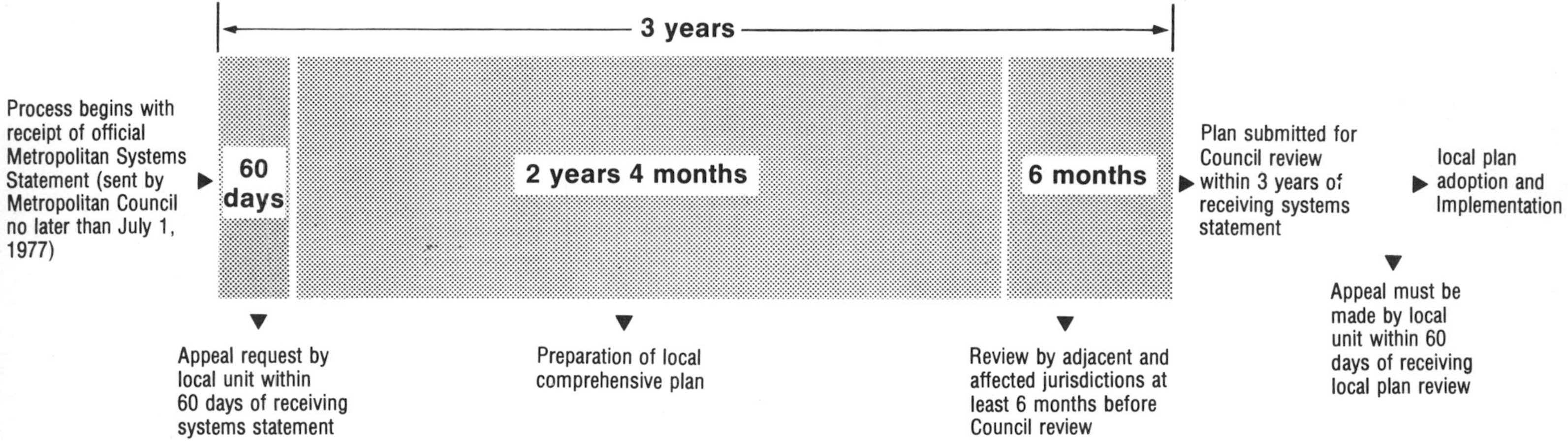

Process begins with receipt of official Metropolitan Systems Statement (sent by Metropolitan Council no later than July 1, 1977)

Appeal request by local unit within 60 days of receiving systems statement

60 days

2 years 4 months

Preparation of local comprehensive plan

3 years

6 months

Review by adjacent and affected jurisdictions at least 6 months before Council review

Plan submitted for Council review within 3 years of receiving systems statement

Appeal must be made by local unit within 60 days of receiving local plan review

local plan adoption and Implementation

Key Dates:

December 31, 1976—By this date each township must decide whether it will prepare its own comprehensive plan or ask the county to do it.

July 1, 1977—Last day for Council transmittal of systems statements.

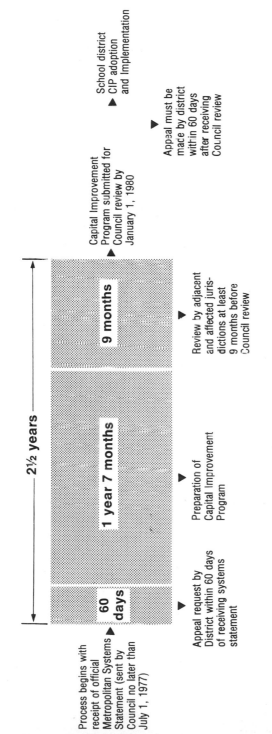

2½ years

60 days

Process begins with receipt of official Metropolitan Systems Statement (sent by Council no later than July 1, 1977)

Appeal request by District within 60 days of receiving systems statement

1 year 7 months

Preparation of Capital Improvement Program

9 months

Review by adjacent and affected jurisdictions at least 9 months before Council review

Capital Improvement Program submitted for Council review by January 1, 1980

Appeal must be made by district within 60 days after receiving Council review

School district CIP adoption and Implementation

Key Dates:

July 1, 1977—Last day for Council transmittal of statements.

January 1, 1980—Capital Improvement Programs submitted for Council review by this date.

August 1976

the Metropolitan Transit Commission (MTC), the Metropolitan Waste Control Commission (MWCC), and the Metropolitan Parks and Open Space Commission (MPOSC). These were placed under close Council supervision by the Legislature in 1974. The Council's controls are of three types. First, it appoints their members, one from each of eight precincts. A precinct, for this purpose, coincides with two Metropolitan Council districts. The term is four years, with half of them expiring every two years. The chairperson of each commission is appointed by the governor with the consent of the Senate, and serves at the governor's pleasure. Second, the Council prepares the general policy plans for waste management, transit, and regional parks. The commissions must then design the development programs to carry out the policies. Of particular importance are the long-range capital expenditures that transform the major plans into reality; these must be specifically approved by the Council, which has the power to direct changes in them. By this means, it gains some control over most major public investments in the region.

In addition to these three metropolitan commissions there are also the *independent metropolitan agencies* which have somewhat greater autonomy: the Metropolitan Airports Commission (MAC), the Metropolitan Mosquito Control District (MMCD), the Metropolitan Sports Facilities Commission (MSFC), the Lake Minnetonka Conservation District, Hennepin County Park Reserve District, and the various watershed and soil-conservation districts. The Council reviews their long-term comprehensive plans and can suspend indefinitely any project that does not conform to Council policies. The Council also examines, and can veto, the major capital expenditure proposals of the MAC. It does not, however, appoint the members of these agencies; most are selected by the governing bodies of the cities and/or counties that overlap them. It can place one of its members in a nonvoting seat on any commission and agency and has done so for the MAC and MMCD. This linkage enables the Council to stay aware of the plans and actions of these agencies.

The Council's control over both kinds of agencies is not concerned with day-to-day operations but with their major plans and expenditures. In the process of establishing this control, it had to win several major disputes. In 1969 and 1970, it vetoed proposals by the Metropolitan Airports Commission to build a second commercial airport at Ham Lake in Anoka County.

A more persistent conflict occurred over transit. As noted in Chapter 2, the 1974 legislative decision not only led to the de facto acceptance of the Metropolitan Council's bus expansion program but it also clarified the Council's policy control over the metropolitan commissions. However, differences in transit philosophy between the Council, the Metropolitan Transit Commission (MTC), and certain key metropolitan legislators remained, and occasional friction was evident during 1975 and 1976. It came to a head in the 1977 session when the Legislature shortened the terms of the four MTC members who had been appointed before the Council gained appointive power. By shortening their terms, the Council was able to appoint their successors, and in July it replaced all four with new members. The newly reconstituted Commission promptly voted to deprive MTC chairman Douglas Kelm of certain procedural and administrative powers. It was clearly a reduction in power and prestige for Kelm. The move was widely interpreted as a victory for the Council and an opportunity for it to exert more immediate control over the MTC. In the future, the Council may be better able to induce the positive action on transit that it desires, as well as veto actions it opposes.

Determining Metropolitan Significance

The Metropolitan Council is authorized by law to review proposed projects or activities of metropolitan special districts, local governments, state agencies, and private enterprises to determine if they are of "metropolitan significance." If it finds that a project has such significance but is not consistent with the *Development Guide* or other policies, it may suspend action on it for up to twelve months. In that time, the Council may negotiate with those responsible for the project and set conditions for removing the suspension. The Council may initiate this review at its own discretion, but it must respond to requests of local governmental units and metropolitan agencies. In addition, review must take place upon petition by a certain number of citizens.

The Council has not used this potentially far-reaching power, owing in part to the difficulty of "drafting definitions that are general enough to cover all the proposals that are potentially of metropolitan significance and at the same time specific enough to provide clear policy to guide the Council in its review process and communicate the 'rules' to project sponsors.'[7] The Council has drafted rules and regulations to define these thresholds of significance, as required by the legislative act, and they are scheduled to go into effect in 1978. These rules stipulate that a project has metropolitan significance if, for example, it would lead to the discharge of more than 50,000 gallons of sewage per day, generate 10,000 vehicle trips per day, or substantially affect any regional park or airport, existing or planned.

Reviewing Grant Applications

The fifth power of the Metropolitan Council is to review applications from local governments and private sources for a wide variety of federal and state government grants and loan guarantees. Such review of requests for federal assistance is mandated by the A-95 circular described earlier. During the period from October 31, 1975, to the same date in 1976, the Council processed 820 such referrals, compared to 770 during the previous twelve months.[8] The applications were addressed to thirteen different federal departments and independent agencies, and to five units of state government. The programs to be funded thereby included practically every kind of physical facility and human service aid established by Congress.

When it receives an application, the Council has a range of options, including immediate approval, approval after modification, outright disapproval, or no comment. This judgment must take into consideration the consistency of the proposed project with the *Development Guide* and other Council policies. Since the federal and state agencies usually accept the recommendations of the reviewing bodies, this gives the Council considerable leverage in getting local units and private enterprises to adhere to its standards. Although most A-95 review agencies have applied this power very timidly and perfunctorily approve nearly all grant applications,[9] the Metropolitan Council has given unconditional endorsement to only about half the requests reaching it. Of 801 applications for federal assistance that the Council actually sent to Washington with its comments during 1975-76, 52 percent had been approved outright, another 40 percent were approved with some question, condition, or amendment, and the remaining 8 percent drew critical comment or disapproval.[10] The only comprehensive study of its use of the A-95 power indicates that it indeed seeks to enforce *Development Guide* policies thereby.[11] In 1973, for example, the Council held up an application for a federal parks grant in order to convince the officials of Golden Valley to plan for more low- and moderate-income housing. This action supported its policy of increasing the proportion of subsidized housing built in the suburbs as compared with the central cities.

The Council also uses the A-95 process to induce local governments to do their own planning. When an application arrives from a particular city or county, the Council staff checks it for consistency not only with the metropolitan plans but also with that unit's own comprehensive plan. Approval of such requests has been less readily given if that community has not done its own planning first.[12]

The Council's experience with the A-95 process indicates that not all the mandated procedures are being followed.[13] First, some federal agencies are accepting and processing grant applications that the applicant never referred to the Council although A-95 requires that they be so processed. This is especially true for human resource programs of the Department of Health, Education and Welfare, which has not fully accepted the A-95 procedure. The Department of Housing and Urban Development, by contrast, has a much better record of compliance. Second, the Council receives very little useful feedback from the federal agencies about their actions on the grant applications. The A-95 circular specifies that such information shall be sent to the regional clearinghouse within seven days of the final decision. When it is not sent, the Council is deprived of an informational tool for evaluating both the effects of its recommendations and the overall pattern of federal grants in the region. A further shortcoming lies in the Council's lack of a policy base for reviewing many human-service program applications and the shortage of staff for investigating the many grant requests as thoroughly as may be needed. The policy base problem is gradually being met by efforts to formulate a social framework that integrates social-service policies and plans in a consistent manner.

Coordinating Aid for Parks and Housing

The sixth role of the Metropolitan Council is to administer and coordinate programs of aid to local governments for housing and parks. The Legislature authorized it in 1974 to act as a Metropolitan Housing and Redevelopment Authority (HRA) in those communities that want federally subsidized housing but do not choose to establish an HRA of their own. The Council has used this power to provide significant amounts of housing for persons of low and moderate income in more than fifty suburban and outlying rural communities. The metropolitan HRA also transmits funds from the Minnesota Housing Finance Agency to low-income homeowners in sixty-two cities for improvement and rehabilitation of their dwellings. For those cities and counties with their own HRAs, the Council gives advice and assistance as needed and trains their staff members. This rare example of intergovernmental housing cooperation has generated considerable interest in the U.S. Department of Housing and Urban Development, paying off in an additional 3.6 million dollars for the Council to distribute.[14]

The Council also received authority in 1974 from the Legislature to borrow 40 million dollars for making grants to local units to acquire parklands. In 1977, this was increased by another 23 million dollars financed by state bonds. To the end of 1976, more than 10,000 acres had been bought.[15] The Council and MPOSC cooperate to prepare regional recreational open space and capital-improvement plans to which these acquisitions must conform. Management and maintenance of each park remains with the city or county in which it is located. By this partnership, the Council is able to work with local authorities to identify space that both levels would like to preserve for public recreational use and to buy it before it is preempted by private developers.

Providing General Research and Assistance

Finally, the Metropolitan Council performs a series of other functions more typical of metropolitan planning agencies elsewhere. It has a broad mandate to research matters of metropolitan concern and make recommendations to the Legislature and other bodies. During 1975 and 1976, it has examined such issues as the preservation of prime agricultural land in the region, the use of pyrolysis to generate fuel from solid waste and sewage sludge, water-quality improvement, the need for bridges across the Minnesota River, and the use of a single region-wide telephone number for emergency calls. Early in 1977, it published *State of the Region*, an extensive compilation of the data it judged necessary to monitor the area's development and change—social, economic, physical, and governmental. These studies supply raw material for future policy initiatives and proposals.

The Council may also, at the request of local governments, assist them in their own planning efforts, from the preparation of comprehensive land-use plans to the drafting of capital-improvement financing programs. It is also empowered to facilitate efforts toward annexations and consolidations of local units and interlocal cooperation on shared problems. For smaller communities that lack professional planning staff, this assistance is especially significant. Finally, the Council may provide legal assistance to local units in disputes arising from their efforts to impose land-use controls that are consistent with the metropolitan policies. It aided Marshan Township (in Dakota County) to make a successful appeal of a lower-court ruling on the constitutionality of an interim building moratorium, and in 1977 worked with the city of Dayton in defending its building-density restrictions in an environmental "critical area" near the Mississippi River. Dayton lost that contest, however.

Conclusion

From the preceding, it is apparent that the Twin Cities Metropolitan Council is an extraordinary metropolitan organization. With its emphasis on policy making and coordination, it is not a general-purpose government such as those created in Nashville, Jacksonville, and Miami. With its own form of representing geographic subareas of the metropolis rather than local governments, it has avoided the major weakness that has paralyzed most councils of government. In some COGs, local member governments have been able to withhold voluntary contributions, effectively veto plans they disliked, and generally prevent the COG from taking effective action.[16] Not only has the Metropolitan Council evolved into a viable organization, it has been given substantial power to act in the seven broad areas of authority outlined above.

What the Council has done with these powers is a major question. Has this all amounted to much sound and fury that signifies nothing? Or is the Council making substantive accomplishments with its powers? These questions will be addressed in the next three chapters.

CHAPTER 4

Physical Development Policies

The Central Role of the Metropolitan Council
in Regional Policy Making

As noted in earlier chapters, Minnesota has opted for a metropolitan public service system that separates policy making from the actual delivery of services. As the central policy-making agency, the Metropolitan Council establishes the policies through the *Metropolitan Development Guide*. As of mid-1977, thirteen chapters of the *Development Guide* have been adopted.

Although the *Metropolitan Development Guide* constitutes the central compendium of metropolitan policies, three characteristics of metropolitan policies make it hard for the average citizen to read individual *Guide* chapters and obtain a clear idea of what is actually taking place. First, there is a confusing combination of specific policies that can be immediately implemented and more general goals that represent ideals which may never be fully attainable. For example, the *Development Guide* chapter on recreation is so specific that it identifies particular sites that will be developed as regional parks. Most of these sites are readily obtainable, and some of them have already been acquired and developed. In contrast to this very specific kind of directive, the health chapter includes a policy stating that "all persons must be able to retain their sense of human dignity in health care settings."[1] Such an ideal may or may not be at-

65

tainable, but it is hard to imagine that public authorities will spend much time checking what constitutes human dignity and if receptionists, nurses, doctors, and nursing-home administrators are treating each of their patients with sufficient dignity. Because of this contrast between highly specific directives and extremely broad goal statements in the *Development Guide* chapters, it becomes impossible for the citizen to read the chapters and be able to distinguish between policies that are actually intended to be implemented and those that were included simply as symbolic ideals meant to pacify strong-minded persons who had input into the chapter-drafting process.

A second problem confronting the citizen trying to understand metropolitan policies is that they are constantly in flux. *Development Guide* chapters are periodically rewritten as new policies replace old ones. Early chapters tend to state general goals which become highly specific in the revised chapters. The first health chapter adopted in 1973, for example, contained only 73 pages and bears little obvious resemblance to the most recent chapter, adopted in 1977, containing over 300 pages. Some chapters simply disappear. The 1971 chapter on diversified centers, for example, was superseded by the 1975 Development Framework chapter.[2] This process of flux is necessary to keep policy planning up-to-date, but it makes it hard for the citizen to distinguish between policies currently in force and those that are being changed or replaced.

A third problem facing the citizen trying to understand metropolitan policies stems from the multiplicity of policy-making actors and extreme functional specialization. Perhaps one reason for the vagueness of so many policies in the *Metropolitan Development Guide* is its attempt to relate to all of these actors. They include the State Legislature, most state executive departments and agencies, the counties, municipalities, special districts and other local governments, the United States Congress, a host of federal bureaus, agencies, and departments, and numerous private organizations and agencies. Metropolitan policy making in the Twin Cities is a perfect example of what Morton Grodzins called "marble cake federalism" as distinguished from "layer cake federalism."[3] No longer is it realistic to conceive of federalism as three separate layers—federal, state, and local. Rather, in Twin Cities metropolitan policy making, all three levels are as intricately interwoven as the colors in a marble cake.

Although marble-cake federalism has intricately interwoven the three horizontal layers of government in the policy-making process, an extreme form of functional specialization has separated planners and technocrats into functional categories along vertical lines that Deil S. Wright called "picket fence federalism."[4] Within a given policy-making function, a "federal picket" exists in which specialists at all levels of government interact fairly smoothly with each other but interact minimally with specialists in other areas, generalist policy makers, and private citizens. Within each "picket," functional fiefdoms have been created analogous to the geographic fiefdoms of the Middle Ages.[5] For private citizens, the net impact of marble-cake and picket-fence federalism has been to make the federal system comprehensible only if they exert great effort.

In health care, for example, a functional fiefdom exists in which specialists in the legislative committees, the national, state, and county health departments, the Metropolitan Health Board planners, and the private health-care providers (hospitals, doctors, and nursing-home administrators) all speak a common jargon. Not only is this jargon alien to the average citizen, it also is not very meaningful to the other Metropolitan Council planning specialists who are busy working in their own functional fiefdoms such as transit, water resources, sewers, solid waste, or parks and recreation. Policy planners tend to specialize by functional area, so there is little cross-fertilization of ideas. As the members of the Metropolitan Council have discovered, the task of interrelating all these actors and functional specialists in order to understand the overall policy framework is an enormous task. The average citizen who casually stops in for one of the Thursday afternoon Metropolitan Council meetings will suddenly face an incomprehensible language filled with terms such as A-95, Section 8, Section 201, Section 208, HSA, MUSA, and, of course, the acronyms of a bewildering variety of agencies that thrive on this jargon—MTC, MWCC, MAC, MPCA, MHB, EQC, EPA, DOT, and MnDOT. The average citizen who cannot devote much time to following the constantly changing functional jargon is likely to find it impossible to grasp the overall policies. At best, he or she may be appointed to one of the many task forces or advisory committees and come to grips with a specific funtional fiefdom. But that is hardly sufficient to obtain a broad understanding of metropolitan policies.

This and the following chapter provide a broad overview that gives a minimal introduction to the jargon of the functional specialists. Following are the categories chosen for analyzing policies: (1) the Development Framework, (2) the physical systems plans, (3) the financial investment framework, (4) the environmental management policies, and (5) the social framework. Although specific policies within these five categories will constantly change, the categories themselves are likely to persist as the overall framework within which metropolitan policy making will occur for many years to come. Focusing on the process by which policies are implemented in these five categories will undoubtedly do some injustice to the timeliness and specificity important to the functional planners, but it will permit a discussion broad enough to provide the average citizen with the overall thrust of what the Metropolitan Council is attempting to accomplish with its various policies. This thrust seems likely to remain valid into the early 1980s. This chapter focuses on the "metropolitan systems" policies that are central to the effort to guide and meet the service needs of the urban growth that is expected to take place.

The Development Framework

The Development Framework was adopted in 1975 as a keystone chapter in the *Metropolitan Development Guide*. This plan essentially decides where future growth should occur in the metropolitan area and establishes a framework for tying other policies into this overarching goal.

The Rationale for the Development Framework

In 1975 the Metropolitan Council estimated that the region's population over the following fifteen years would grow by between 500,000 and 800,000 people. The number of jobs was projected to grow by 400,000 and the number of new housing units by 380,000.[6] If this growth continues as it has over the previous two decades, it will be scattered over the seven-county region. Scattered development of this sort produces a series of costs that the Metropolitan Council wishes to avoid. As streets, sewer lines, and transit lines are extended, the costs for these service extensions are borne by the entire metropolitan population in the form of higher taxes and utility fees. As population densities rise in hitherto rural areas, the local governments are pressured to build schools, provide more police and fire protection, and to increase their staff size and budgets. Because scarce public funds have to be used to build these extra sewers, roads, school buildings, and police and fire stations, a social cost is imposed, since less public money will be available to deal with already existing problems.[7] Another cost of scattered urbanization is that it forces people to travel longer distances to work, shop, and use other services. Premature development often eats up potential parkland. The historic practice of ignoring septic-tank regulations, which in Minnesota have been weak to begin with, has in the past led to the pollution of the groundwater supply. As the Council examined all these costs of scattered urban development, it concluded that up to 2 billion dollars in public expenditures could be avoided if the expected urban growth from 1975 to 1990 were channeled into predetermined areas.

What the Development Framework Does

The Development Framework has several goals. These include channeling growth into predetermined areas, preserving the integrity of the natural environment, expanding social choices available to the population, reducing the concentrations of low-income residents in certain neighborhoods, encouraging diversified economic growth in the region, providing an equitable system of financing public services, and stimulating citizen involvement in the governmental process.

In the Council's mind, channeling future growth is the key to attaining all the other goals. As shown in Figure 4-1, the Development Framework divides the region into five distinct planning areas: (1) the two centers of the metropolitan region, (2) the fully developed areas, (3) the area of planned urbanization, (4) the freestanding growth centers, and (5) the rural service area.

The first three areas constitute the Metropolitan Urban Services Area (MUSA), and the perimeter of this area is called the MUSA line. Although the map indicates fairly definite boundaries for the MUSA line, the boundaries will not actually be finalized until the individual municipalities have the chance to develop their own land-use plans and submit them to the Council for review. Outside the MUSA line

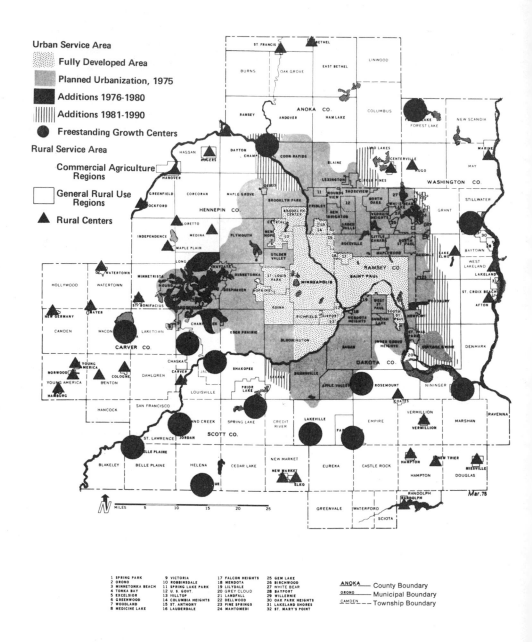

Legend (map key):

Urban Service Area
- Fully Developed Area
- Planned Urbanization, 1975
- Additions 1976-1980
- Additions 1981-1990
- Freestanding Growth Centers

Rural Service Area
- Commercial Agriculture Regions
- General Rural Use Regions
- Rural Centers

1 SPRING PARK
2 ORONO
3 MINNETONKA BEACH
4 TONKA BAY
5 EXCELSIOR
6 GREENWOOD
7 WOODLAND
8 MEDICINE LAKE
9 VICTORIA
10 ROBBINSDALE
11 SPRING LAKE PARK
12 U. S. GOVT.
13 HILLTOP
14 COLUMBIA HEIGHTS
15 ST. ANTHONY
16 LAUDERDALE
17 FALCON HEIGHTS
18 MENDOTA
19 LILYDALE
20 GREY CLOUD
21 LANDFALL
22 DELLWOOD
23 PINE SPRINGS
24 MAHTOMEDI
25 GEM LAKE
26 BIRCHWOOD
27 WHITE BEAR
28 BAYPORT
29 WILLERNIE
30 OAK PARK HEIGHTS
31 LAKELAND SHORES
32 ST. MARY'S POINT

ANOKA — County Boundary
ORONO — Municipal Boundary
CAMDEN --- Township Boundary

Figure 4-1. Development Framework planning areas.
Courtesy of the Metropolitan Council.

and the fourteen freestanding growth centers will be the rural service area. The rural service area is to be used primarily for agriculture, and extensive development will not be permitted there. For each of these five areas the Council has indicated a different set of objectives.

The Metropolitan Centers and the Fully Developed Areas

The Metropolitan Centers comprise the central business districts of Minneapolis and St. Paul plus nearby areas such as the state capitol, Cedar-Riverside, and the University of Minnesota, which house a variety of activities and services. The fully developed areas comprise the remaining portion of the two central cities plus the inner-ring suburbs that have no extensive remaining developable land. The major problem in these areas is that a climate of uncertainty prevents the retention and influx of private industries and middle-class people that would stabilize old neighborhoods, create a more heterogeneous population, revitalize commercial areas, and take advantage of the available housing stock. Council policies for the fully developed areas deal directly with these problems. They seek to encourage more private investment, reduce crime, improve educational and other public services, encourage neighborhood improvement associations, reduce the concentration of poor people in certain neighborhoods, provide conditions for middle-income people to move into the housing, rebuild selected commercial areas, and plan for the use of the remaining environmentally significant areas, such as the Mississippi River shorelines.

Until recently, however, the Council has not moved decisively to implement these policies.[8] Because the critical sewage and other metropolitan-growth problems that led to the creation of the Council were primarily suburban problems, the Council produced few specific policy recommendations for redevelopment in the central cities. The central-city governments in turn tended to ignore the Council and were at best ambivalent toward it. Perhaps because Council decisions on sewers, airports, open space, and guiding future growth impinged much more directly on the suburbs than on the central cities, the Minneapolis and St. Paul city governments had much less need than the suburban governments to worry about policy decisions made by the Metropolitan Council.

In 1976 a Citizens League Committee called for greater attention to redevelopment in the central cities. In the same year the Council created a Task Force for the Fully Developed Areas. The task force recommended a "New Urban Policy" that would unite public and private initiatives to maintain, reuse, and redevelop existing facilities in the metropolitan centers. The Council in 1977 adopted some of these recommendations as amendments to the Development Framework. However, it is still not clear how the Council can translate these policies into practice. The "New Urban Policy" recommendations, like the earlier fully developed area section of the Development Framework, deal less with practical programs than they do with general philosophy, broad goals, and guidelines for planning. Indeed, the land-use planning procedures established to implement the Development Framework are directed overwhelmingly at the rural area and the areas of planned urbanization rather than at the central cities. For all these reasons, advocates of redeveloping the central cities will have to maintain a critical scrutiny of the Council's efforts to implement its goals for the fully developed areas.

The Area of Planned Urbanization

Since most of the future population growth will be in this area, the Council views it as critical. The Council seeks to contain the expansion of urban services within this area and the freestanding growth centers and to reduce reliance on the automobile. Through the land-use planning process established in 1976 it will oblige the development plans of counties and municipalities to locate future growth within the MUSA line and provide for the efficient use of existing facilities. This need is most obvious in the educational sector. Declining enrollment in some school districts is forcing them to close school buildings, while neighboring districts only a few miles away are constructing new school buildings to accommodate their growing population. Cities in the areas of planned urbanization are also directed to provide housing for low-income people and to concentrate new commercial construction near major diversified centers that have been identified by the *Metropolitan Development Guide.*

The Freestanding Growth Centers

To channel growth into fourteen centers beyond the MUSA line, the Council will support urban services such as sewers, roads, and transit in these centers. It encourages orderly annexation of townships to the growth centers as their populations begin to exceed their municipal boundaries. These centers must also develop land-use plans consistent with the overall objectives of the *Metropolitan Development Guide.*

The Rural Service Area

Primary land use for this area is agricultural. Metropolitan urban services such as sewers and transit will not be made available to this area. Each community within the rural service area is required to draft a land-use plan that recognizes its essential rural or small-town nature.

How the Development Framework Will Be Implemented

The major tool for implementing the Development Framework is the land-planning process established in 1976 and discussed in Chapter 3. In accord with the 1976 Land Planning Act, systems plans have been drafted for each of the four metropolitan services (sewers, transit, parks, and airports) indicating where, when, and under what conditions these services will be extended through the metropolis. These systems plans will be discussed in greater detail later. Basically, the assumption behind the Council's thinking is that development is not likely to occur in areas that are denied sewers, bus service, and roads. Hence the supply and denial of these services can be used as tools to implement the Development Framework.

In addition to this major tool for implementing the Development Framework, a number of other devices either exist or are being proposed. To help local governments preserve the rural service area for agriculture, the Council has prepared an *Agriculture Planning Handbook.*[9] The Legislature in 1967 enacted the Green Acres Law, which permits farmland in urbanizing areas to be assessed and taxed below its market value. However, if a farmer accepts the lower tax rate and subsequently develops the land, he or she must pay back the difference in taxes for the preceding three years. This plan is not working as well as was originally hoped. There is some feeling that it is contributing to the spiraling costs of farmland and that it may be helping developers and speculators more than farmers. The Metropolitan Council staff is studying ways to improve the act.

A second supplementary device for preserving the agricultural areas is the Council's urging of the Minnesota Pollution Control Agency (MPCA) to upgrade septic-tank regulations and inspections. This is being considered by the MPCA, but the proposed regulations are going to be "non-mandatory," which will be a serious weakness in implementing the Development Framework. To compensate for this weakness the Metropolitan Council is considering directing the Metropolitan Waste Control Commission to establish its own mandatory septic-tank regulations within the seven-county region.

In addition to these tools for implementation, the Council is also seeking to establish a metropolitan development fund with revolving assets of 25 million dollars to assist the projects that would give a particular boost to the Development Framework. The *Development Guide* plan also called for a metropolitan land bank, but that has never gotten beyond the discussion stage. Finally, the Council has supported the establishment of municipal development corporations to help achieve overall development goals.[10]

The Physical Systems Plans for the Metropolis

As discussed in Chapter 3, the 1976 Land Planning Act required systems plans to be drafted for the four physical services of sewers, transportation, parks, and airports. The first three of these systems plans are viewed as critical for the implementation of the Development Framework. Because sewers, transit, and parks in particular play important roles in shaping the growth of the metropolis, and are critical to implementing the Development Framework, each is worth examining in some detail.

Sewer Policies for the Metropolis

The metropolitan sewerage plan seeks to attain two objectives. First, as indicated earlier, it is seen as a tool for implementing the Development Framework. Second, the sewerage system is also seen as the primary means of bringing the quality of regional rivers and lakes up to the standards established by the Minnesota Pollution Control Agency (MPCA) and the 1972 Federal Water Pollution Control Act.[11]

In accord with the Development Framework, a new metropolitan sewer service boundary has been drawn, roughly coinciding with the MUSA line. With a few exceptions, the fully developed areas within this line will be tied into the centrally controlled sewer system. Sewer line interceptors will connect all but three of the freestanding growth centers into the system. As the areas of planned urbanization are developed, all but a few of them will also be phased into the central sewer system. The local governments must submit a sewer plan to the MWCC. They may continue to own their sewage collection facilities, but all interceptors and waste-treatment plants within the metropolitan sewer service boundary will be owned and operated by the MWCC. Factories, shopping centers, schools, and other nonmunicipal institutions that have their own treatment plants may choose to either bring them up to MPCA standards or tie into the new MWCC system.

The rural areas will not be tied into the system. Small towns that have not been designated as freestanding growth centers may operate their own treatment plants, but they must meet MPCA standards and will not receive any direct financial aid. Even though the large interceptors that connect the freestanding growth centers with the urban service area run through rural areas, Metropolitan Council policies prohibit future subdivision developments along these interceptors from tying into the main system.

Development will not be prohibited in the rural areas, but the Council hopes to limit the density of this rural development by imposing stricter septic-tank regulations. However, as indicated earlier, these regulations will be nonmandatory, thus weakening the Development Framework.

The sewer system is also vital for achieving the water-quality standards established by the state of Minnesota and the federal 1972 Water Pollution Control Act. The MPCA has established six water-quality classifications and identified the water-quality standards that apply to each of the six rivers in the metropolitan region into which treated waste effluent is discharged. The MWCC discharges are required to meet standards that will help bring those water courses up to the desired levels.[12] As the MWCC over the past seven years has eliminated the many separate municipal treatment plants and centralized treatment into a limited number of well-maintained MWCC facilities, the quality of these streams has improved considerably.[13]

The implementation process for the sewer policies was established by the 1974 Metropolitan Reorganization Act. Under the terms of that act, the Metropolitan Council was made responsible for developing a sewer policy for the metropolitan area, determining where the sewer lines would be extended, and deciding which communities would be allowed to tie into the system. The MWCC is to develop a five-year capital improvement program to implement the overall policy and submit its capital budget to the Council for approval. Before the 1974 act, there were periodic conflicts and misunderstandings between the Council and the MWCC (at that time called the Metropolitan Sewer Board) over division of powers and planning responsibilities. Most of these misunderstandings were resolved by the Reorganization Act, and sewer planning has proceeded much more smoothly since.[14]

Transportation Policies

Transportation planning has been the most conflict ridden of all the metropolitan policy-making areas. Almost since the creation of the Metropolitan Council there have been serious political conflicts over airports, highways, and, above all, transit. Completion of the region's interstate highway network has been stalled by an effectively organized citizen and legislative opposition. The Council and the Metropolitan Transit Commission (MTC) have repeatedly been at odds over transit development and personality differences between their leaders.

Many of the increments in the Council's responsibilities have involved transportation planning, and its policies have largely been forged in these recurring conflicts. In Chapter 2, the 1973 clash between the Council and the MTC was surveyed, out of which came both the Metropolitan Reorganization Act and the present reliance on bus transit. In essence, that act confirmed the Council's power to do overall transportation planning, leaving the MTC responsible for programs to implement the plans. Even so, the MTC and its chairman, Douglas Kelm, have not been reluctant to press their viewpoints, even when they clash with Council thinking.

The current policy plan for transportation is stated in the *Development Guide* chapter adopted in 1976.[15] Its basic objective is to secure more efficient use of existing transportation investments, both public and private. This calls for strategies to encourage people to ride to their destinations, whether in a bus or a privately owned vehicle, rather than drive a car alone. It views the public and private sectors as equally important providers of *transit*, defining that term simply as ridership. Because the Twin Cities metropolitan area is so large and decentralized, the Council acknowledges that no single mode of transit will serve it adequately. Thus, a plan must provide for availability of various modes, meeting the mobility needs of working commuters and the handicapped, of the high-density neighborhoods and the suburban communities. Throughout, stress falls on using transit modes that require little or no additional public investment.

To identify these diverse transportation needs more clearly, the Council divided the metropolitan area into twelve subregions. Travel-behavior analyses have indicated that most trips are for less than five miles and tend to fall within the boundaries of those subregions. Each subregion contains the basic necessities for daily living, accessible by such short trips. The transit plan emphasizes improving opportunities to ride within the subregions and decreasing reliance on private cars for these short distances. It calls, also, for express bus service between the subregions and to the Minneapolis and St. Paul central business districts.

One section of the plan sets forth the highway system as it is to be in 1990. When completed, it will have 346 miles of principal arterial highways and 245 miles of intermediate arterials. This is 112 miles less than planned in the 1972 transportation chapter, a reduction owing to lower growth projections, more emphasis on transit, and greater expected efficiency in the system's usage.

The transit section of the plan is concerned with the vehicles that use the highways and streets to transport persons other than the drivers. Standard-size buses and minibuses have their places, along with "paratransit" — commuter vans, car pools, taxis, demand-responsive buses, and innovative small-vehicle systems for circulation within the two downtown areas. The major criteria for choosing the mode for a given type of service are reliability and low cost.

The implementation of this transportation plan involves several agencies. The highway plan will become reality through the efforts of the Minnesota Department of Transportation (MnDOT) and the seven-county highway departments. Much of the funding for major highways comes from the Federal Highway Administration, but route choice, construction, and maintenance are the state's responsibility. The MnDOT must submit an annual highway improvement program to the Metropolitan Council for review and comment. It is also charged to study the "trouble spots" on the metropolitan interstate highway system and explore ways to give preferential treatment on highways to multi-passenger vehicles such as car pools, commuter vans, and buses.

Implementing the transit portion of the plan is the responsibility of the MTC. Since assuming ownership of the Twin City Lines in 1970, it has achieved a ridership increase of about 40 percent while keeping the basic fare at thirty cents. Since its plan for a rail rapid-transit system was blocked by the Metropolitan Council and the Legislature in 1973, it has moved slowly toward experimenting with the paratransit service outlined in the policy plan. There have been experiments with dial-a-ride buses, special origin-to-destination service for the handicapped, and neighborhood circulation in the suburban cities of Hopkins and White Bear Lake. Some paratransit plans are difficult to implement owing to high costs and opposition from the transit workers' union.

The Legislature chose in 1971 to begin public subsidy of metropolitan transit service, and the gap between operating costs and passenger revenues widened to 26 million dollars by 1976. Since the Legislature appropriated funds to cover this subsidy and authorized its modest property tax levy, its choices directly influence the MTC's ability to respond to the Metropolitan Council's policies. As an incentive to greater efficiency, the state, beginning in 1978, will guarantee the MTC a subsidy of forty-eight cents per passenger carried rather than a flat sum. There will also be additional grants to make up the cost of reduced "social fares" for the elderly, handicapped, and young. In addition, the MnDOT will finance experimental bus and paratransit programs in the state, and the MTC may receive as much as 2 million dollars for this in 1978-79. This amounts to a "go ahead" on implementing the Council's policies, but with a signal to avoid letting the subsidies increase too rapidly. The immediate net impact has been a cutback on bus service to outlying suburbs and a reduction in the number of bus drivers employed by the MTC.[16]

In 1977 the U.S. Urban Mass Transportation Administration gave preliminary approval to funding a small-vehicle people-mover system for downtown St. Paul. This rail line would run at underground and above-street levels, connecting the central business district with the state capitol, the civic center, and the cathedral on Ramsey Hill. The MTC supports the project and has conducted initial studies on it. But the Metropolitan Council has doubts about its economic feasibility and the likelihood of its revitalizing central St. Paul. The Legislature, which was asked to authorize the MTC's contribution of 10 percent of the project costs, also was unsure, but it did give it just enough to continue planning until a final decision comes from Washington. If built, the people mover will be a critical experiment in using improved transit to draw more business and residential investment into the central city, and a test of the Council's policy for downtown circulation systems.

It is also important that several legislators have called for cutbacks on service to some of the outlying suburbs. This development has two very important implications. First, it provides added support for the rationale behind the Council's Development Framework. Unless suburban sprawl is contained, it will become exceedingly expensive to provide transit service to all portions of the urbanized region. Second, as the MTC chairman argued, some kind of subsidy is required to meet the Metropolitan Council's policy of providing access to transit to all residents of the metropolitan area.[17] According to some observers, typical transit owners were historically real-estate entrepreneurs who built transit lines to increase the value of their real-estate holdings. The profits on real-estate development subsidized their transit operations. When the real-estate holdings became fully developed, the entrepreneurs usually stopped subsidizing their transit operations, cut back on service, and often appealed to their cities to bail them out.[18] Public agencies such as the MTC cannot, of course, use their transit system to increase the value of their real-estate holdings. At best, they can use a value-capture tax to extract some of the increase in value that their operations bring to certain property owners. Other than this, the Twin Cities must anticipate substantial subsidies to transit well into the forseeable future if the area is going to continue to receive the kind of service provided over the past decade and envisioned in the Metropolitan Council policies plan for the next decade.

Airport Planning

When the Metropolitan Council rejected the proposal of the Metropolitan Airports Commission (MAC) to build a major commercial airport in the Ham Lake area of Anoka County, it did not have an airports plan of its own. Although this action was taken mainly to protect that environmentally sensitive location, the Council recognized the need for studying the issue and applied for a federal grant to prepare a regional airports plan. Working with the MAC, it produced the airports chapter of the *Development Guide* early in 1973. It called for locating a future commerical airport within a large "search area" in western Anoka County. In addition, the plan established a system to encompass the region's seven airports under the MAC's jurisdiction, plus five private airfields. Each was to have a specific role in meeting the needs of commercial, general, and military aviation. To ensure that the facilities would be available to serve expected growth in air traffic over the next three decades, eight more search areas were designated for future general-service airports.

No action was taken after 1973 to acquire land within the Anoka County search area. Rather, the MAC has expanded the facilities at existing Minneapolis-St. Paul International Airport, and in 1976 proposed to enlarge the annual passenger capacity from 7 million to 34 million and to double the number of flights that could be accommodated. In December 1977, the Metropolitan Council adopted a new *Development Guide* chapter on airports which dropped the earlier plan for an Anoka County commercial airport. However, it stressed the need for new facilities to serve the growing volume of general aviation and directed that searches take place in Hennepin and Dakota counties for two such sites.

Parks and Recreation

Before 1974, the provision of recreation areas in the metropolitan region was quite inconsistent. Although there are in the region about 100 lakes of over 100 acres, not all of them were available for public use. Twenty-seven percent of the lakes had no provision for public access.[19] In terms of park area, the region had about three dozen sizable city and county parks, but their planning and management were not tied together in any systematic way. Minneapolis was blessed with the donation of private land in the late 1800s that resulted in the development of a park system around the city's lake area. St. Paul also had a number of attractive parks. However, many suburbs developed with inadequate attention to recreational needs. Suburban municipalities typically had a subdivision ordinance requiring builders to provide park space for a given number of houses constructed. But the builders were often allowed to avoid this by paying a fixed amount of money into the city's recreation budget.

As a result of this inconsistent recreation planning, no systematic area-wide approach to recreation had ever been undertaken. Using criteria of the National Parks and Recreation Association, the Metropolitan Parks and Open Space Commission (MPOSC) calculated in 1974 that the entire metropolitan area had a deficiency of nearly 7,000 acres of recreation space. Unless new acquisitions were made, that deficiency would grow to over 20,000 acres by 1990.[20]

As an early step in planning for a regional recreation system, the Commission classified nine different recreation open-space categories. Four of these, such as parks or playfields, exist at the neighborhood or community level and are viewed as the exclusive responsibility of the local government. Five categories, however, are regional in scope, and it would be impossible for local governments acting by themselves to create a region-wide systematic plan for them. These five categories are regional parks, regional park reserves, regional trail corridors, regional historic parks, and special-use areas.

Having established these categories, the MPOSC then drew up a plan to acquire enough land over the following twenty years to create a system of metropolitan-wide recreational open space. This plan was adopted by the Metropolitan Council in 1975 as part of the *Metropolitan Development Guide*. The system is designed to add twenty-six new regional parks and park reserves as well as about 525 miles of recreational trail corridors to the existing park space. The regional parks will be located primarily on lakes and rivers to accommodate water sports in summer, and skiing, snowshoeing, and snowmobiling in winter. The regional trails will link the parks and population centers and run along rivers and streams; they are designed for biking, hiking, ski touring, snowmobiling, canoeing, and related activities. These acquisitions will be phased in over a fifteen-year period with the highest priority sites being purchased immediately. By the end of 1977, over 10,500 acres had been acquired.

To fund these recreational areas, the Legislature in 1974 authorized the Metropolitan Council to issue 40 million dollars in park acquisition bonds. To lessen the impact on metropolitan property taxpayers, it provided in subsequent sessions for state assistance in paying off these bonds. In 1977 the Legislature passed a 61 million dollar Omnibus Parks Bill which allotted the Metropolitan Council 22 million dollars for regional parks, 2 million for special use sites, and an additional 3.3 million for regional trails. The 1977 funding differed from the earlier funding in that nearly half the money was earmarked for development rather than acquisition.[21]

As in all the Council's operations, it acts in a middle capacity between the Legislature, state agencies, the Parks and Open Space Commission, and the local governments. Funding and bonding authority are provided by the Legislature. The Council does not purchase land directly or operate any facilities, however. This is done by the counties, park districts, and, in some cases, municipalities that already possess the staff and the competence. The counties are charged with preparing an open-space master plan including a five-year capital-improvement budget for acquisition and development. When the county, the local municipality, and the Metropolitan Council all agree on the site to be purchased, the implementation runs smoothly. But at times bitter conflicts arise. For example, the Council's system plan designates Big Marine Lake in Washington County as a regional park, but the residents of that area protested vehemently against its inclusion. When the Washington County master plan is completed, the Council will examine it carefully to see if it too designates Big Marine Lake as a regional park site. If it does not do so, it will be inconsistent with the Council's system plan for regional parks, and a difficult period of bargaining and negotiating will result to determine who prevails.

A related problem with implementing the system plan is also illustrated by Washington County. Lacking an extensive tax base, that county finds itself hard pressed to pay for the increased costs of operating and maintaining more parks. For this reason, the county may be reluctant to accept Metropolitan Council grants for any additional park acquisitions. As the new regional parks are developed, their operating costs will soar. The Metropolitan Council is currently studying this problem and expects to make future recommendations for some form of state assistance based on state appropriations, users' fees, or perhaps earmarking revenue from watercraft licenses and camping fees.

The role of the Metropolitan Council in the implementation process is to review the open-space master plans of each county and to allocate the park funds to the counties. In doing this, the Metropolitan Council relies heavily on the MPOSC. The Commission meets regularly to update the system plan, study the counties' grant requests for acquisitions, and recommend how the acquisition and development funds will be spent. Although the MPOSC has only advisory powers, its status was upgraded in 1977 when the Legislature authorized its members to receive the same per diem pay as the members of the other metropolitan commissions (MTC, MWCC, and MAC). Unlike the other three commissions, however, the MPOSC does not directly administer its function and relies on the Metropolitan Council for its staff.

The Metropolitan Investment Framework

As noted earlier, one of the major arguments made in favor of adopting the Development Framework was that channeling future growth into the urban-services area would require dramatic extensions of service within the MUSA line and to the freestanding growth centers. If everything projected in the four metropolitan service plans (transportation, sewers, airports, and parks) were to be accomplished, total capital indebtedness of the four metropolitan agencies in charge of these services (MTC, MWCC, MAC and the Metropolitan Council) would more than double to about 683 million dollars by 1990.[22] If such a level were to be reached at the present total of assessed property valuation, the result could make the bond ratings of the metropolitan agencies fall from a AA rating to an A rating. This would result in higher interest rates on any new bonds issued by these agencies.

The question of total indebtedness of government bodies has become of great concern in recent years because of fiscal disasters that occurred in other governments. In New York, the Urban Development Corporation defaulted on its bonds in 1975. The city of New York was saved from defaulting on its bonds only by last-minute bailout actions by the state of New York and the United States government. In Minnesota, fiscal mismanagement in the St. Paul School District caused its bond ratings to drop and brought it to the edge of default. In their recent monograph on the Twin Cities, a team of respected geographers warned that the extensive redevelopment activities in downtown St. Paul and Minneapolis had contributed greatly to increasing the total bonded indebtedness of the Minneapolis-St. Paul area from $67 per capita in 1950 to $256 in 1960, and $598 in 1971. The authors wrote: "The fiscal facts raise questions whether the Twin Cities area, or any other major urban region, can continue making a major business of rebuilding itself. Much of the current rebuilding may be just the lengthened shadow of huge debt-financed capital improvements packed into a short span of years."[23]

Not only have the metropolitan systems plans committed the region to a dramatic increase in total bonded indebtedness, but the projects to be constructed with these capital funds require additional annual revenues to keep them operating and to pay off the debt service. The operating costs and debt service payments of the four metropolitan agencies alone increased from 25 million dollars in 1970 to 90 million in 1975.[24]

At the same time that these increases will occur, federal and state grants to local governments are not expected to keep pace. If one extrapolates existing expenditures and revenue trends into the future, by 1990 a gap of 296 million dollars between expenditures and revenues appears. Clearly, there will be continuing pressure over the next fifteen years to cut back on expenditures and to increase taxes. Since Minnesota is already one of the most highly taxed states, the Council is dubious about the willingness of the metropolitan population to carry an even greater burden.

For all these reasons, the Metropolitan Council in 1977 adopted a Metropolitan Investment Framework that will enable it to exercise some control over these projected expenditures. The Investment Framework consists of twelve policies with three basic objectives. First, beginning in 1978, the Metropolitan Council will produce a biennial report on the impact of fiscal policies of all governments in the region. There are 273 governments in the seven-county area, and their fiscal conditions will be monitored in these biennial reports.

Second, since the Council has direct authority over the four metropolitan systems agencies (MWCC, MTC, MAC, and MPOSC) it will establish a metropolitan-agency budgeting review process. Currently, although the Council reviews the capital budgets of these agencies, their capital projects are not compared with each other.[25] Starting in 1978, this will be done on a biennial basis. As a control measure, the review process will focus on two financial limits. First, a *regional income index* will be calculated from the total of all personal income and the assessed valuation of all taxable property in the region. Ideally, all metropolitan agency revenues will be limited to .8 percent of that amount. Second, with an eye toward maintaining the AA bond rating for the metropolitan agencies, a *metropolitan agency debt indicator* will be calculated. This is the amount of total debt that cannot be exceeded if the bond ratings are to be maintained at AA. Currently, the indicator is at 650 million dollars. But as the property value and income levels of the region rise, the indicator will also go up. The regional income index limit and the metropolitan agency debt indicator limit are not intended as absolute limits beyond which the agencies may not spend. Rather, the Council will use them as criteria for knowing when the agency plans are approaching realistic financial limits.

Third, the Council will concern itself with the investment decisions of local governments. In reviewing their proposals for grants under the A-95 and similar regulations, the Council "will comment on the potential financial impact of the proposal on affected public agencies."[26] This comment will be based on the ability of the community to finance the project and on the need for the project compared with other needs.

By using these three approaches, the Council hopes to have a monitoring device to guide the total amount of public expenditures of the metropolitan systems. At the very least, a mechanism now exists for simultaneously reviewing the capital budgets of the three metropolitan commissions, for forcing some consideration of overall financial constraints on the review process, and for forcing some consideration of operations and maintenance expenses when capital-spending decisions are made.

Conclusion

Through its Development Framework, its physical systems plans, and its investment framework, the Metropolitan Council has attempted to produce a systematic design for guiding the physical expansion of the metropolitan region. Furthermore, through the Metropolitan Reorganization Act of 1974, the land-planning process established in 1976, and the authority to determine matters of metropolitan significance, the Minnesota Legislature has also given the Council an impressive array of tools to accomplish its growth-control objectives. The tools are probably more far reaching than the growth-control powers given to any other metropolitan body in the United States. Whether these powers are commensurate with the task, however, is a very important question that observers will be asking over the next decade. This question will be examined in Chapter 6. Before doing that, we shall discuss in Chapter 5 the en-environmental protection and social policies of the Council.

CHAPTER 5

Improving the Quality of Life

In the preceding chapter we analyzed Metropolitan Council policies for controlling the physical growth of the metropolis. In this chapter we examine policies for improving the quality of life. These are not mutually exclusive categories; the quality of life in the Twin Cities metropolitan area depends in great measure on the success of the policies discussed here—those for environmental protection and those dealing with social problems.

Environmental Protection Policies

The Metropolitan Council has devoted considerable attention to developing policies to protect and improve the overall natural environment of the seven-county region. In fact, the major force leading to the creation of the Council in 1967 was the breakdown of the existing sewage systems and the resulting threat to the water supply. The Council's first policies dealt with the sewage problem, which was discussed earlier. Subsequent environmental protection policies focused on solid-waste management, hazardous waste disposal, and water-resource management.

As in other policy arenas, the Metropolitan Council functions as the regional policy-making body and implementation is left to other agencies. In sewers and hazardous waste disposal, the Metropolitan

87

Waste Control Commission is the implementing agency. For other solid-waste management, the counties are the key agencies. And in water-resources management, as will be discussed later, implementation is divided piecemeal among a number of different governments.

Solid-Waste Management Policies

Sanitary Landfills

The Council's original chapter on solid-waste disposal was adopted in 1970. At that time the Council opted for a solid-waste disposal plan that relied exclusively on sanitary landfill techniques. Incineration as a disposal technique was rejected, because its cost was estimated to be almost twice as high as that of sanitary landfills.[1] Recycling and resource-recovery techniques were also rejected. They were thought to be too expensive and not yet technologically feasible.

Accordingly, the Council adopted a set of rigorous policies designed to produce an environmentally sound disposal system. The landfills were to be run by the county governments, and the solid-waste collection was to be left to contractual relationships between municipalities and privately owned refuse haulers. At the time, sixty-two landfill operations existed in the seven-county region, and sixty of these were determined to be "unsanitary operations."[2] All were obliged to "comply with the new standards or cease operations."[3] As a result of these guidelines, by June 1976 the number of licensed sanitary landfills had declined from sixty-two to eleven.

Although the Council in 1970 rejected recycling and resource-recovery methods of solid-waste disposal, it recognized that technological advances in these fields were proceeding rapidly. Thus, it designed its 1970 landfill system plan for no more than a ten-year period. As a result of this limited approach, the eleven licensed landfills will be totally filled by the early 1980s. They will then have to be expanded or new sites will have to be identified.

Reduction of Solid Waste

Although available landfill space is disappearing, the solid waste being generated is growing faster than the population. In 1968, 1.1 million tons of municipal refuse were generated, an average of 3.2 pounds per capita per day.[4] By 1974, this had risen to 1.674 million tons, an average of 4.4 pounds per capita per day. And by 1990, total municipal waste is projected to equal 2.432 million tons annually, or 5.2 pounds per person per day.[5] This does not include wastes such as tree removal, street sweepings, or construction and demolition debris that are not collected through the municipal collection systems. Municipal waste accounts for about half of all wastes.

It is clear from these figures that less landfill space would be needed if the total amount of solid wastes generated could be substantially reduced. However, if serious reductions of solid waste are to be achieved, there will have to be far-reaching changes in the "throwaway" mentality and modes of operation of both consumers and industries. Product lifetimes will have to be extended, and the amount of energy and materials used per product reduced. Obviously, the Metropolitan Council cannot produce social changes of such magnitude. Although the Legislature has enacted some provisions for establishing standards for packaging containers, it, too, has only limited ability to alter people's values. Consequently, the Metropolitan Council views waste reduction and conservation programs as "worthy long-range goals," while recognizing that the Council itself is not in a position "to regulate or otherwise establish and implement major waste reductions programs."[6]

Resource Recovery

The exhaustion of current landfill space also increased the attractiveness of experimenting with recycling techniques. In 1976, the Minnesota Legislature passed the Solid Waste Recovery Act which for the first time provides incentives for developing resource-recovery facilities. The major incentive was authorizing the metropolitan counties to issue bonds to raise capital for constructing resource-recovery facilities. These bonds will not have to be approved by the voters in an election. This act made it feasible for the first time to invest substantial sums in recycling, and it obliged the Metropolitan Council to develop policies to license and regulate the resource-recovery plants. In November 1976 the Council drafted a number of resource-recovery policies which were added as amendments to the solid waste chapter in the *Guide*.

These policies cover two types of resource recovery. First, combustible waste material (about 80 percent of the total) can be burned to produce heat and electricity. This heat and electricity in turn can be sold to industries and other consumers in the vicinity of the resource-recovery plant. It is estimated that combustible wastes have about half the BTU value of coal. Given the shortages of natural gas and petroleum that face the Upper Midwest region in the coming years, this may become a very valuable use of solid waste. The second type of resource recovery focuses on recycleable materials — on the 20 percent of the solid waste that consists of recycleable materials such as glass, ferrous metals, and nonferrous metals.

The 1976 Solid Waste Act which gave counties the bonding authority to finance waste-recovery facilities also obliged the Metropolitan Council to approve any such facilities financed through public funds and to establish the criteria and standards that would be used to determine approval or disapproval. Council approval would not be needed for exclusively private facilities operating in traditional recycling fields such as aluminum, waste paper, scrap metal, or junked cars. Although no public solid-waste resource-recovery facilities have yet been constructed or licensed under the 1976 legislation, the Council has adopted a set of criteria and standards which suggest the general characteristics these plants are likely to assume. First, they will be big, because the Council has determined that they must optimize economies of scale. Preferences will be given to plants that have the capacity to process 500 tons of waste per day.[7] Second, although they will be publicly financed from revenue bonds, the intent is to turn them over to private operators. Finally, since the Council has to approve long-range contracts between the plants and municipalities that will supply the waste, the Council is likely to use this authority to ensure that the plants are spaced among the various waste-disposal districts that will be established.[8]

Although the public will be involved in financing the recovery plants, the Metropolitan Council has adopted a number of criteria that minimize the possibility of the plants becoming a burden to taxpayers. First, it encourages the use of revenue bonds rather than general obligation bonds to construct the facilities. General obligation bonds are a debt of the issuing government and a property tax may be levied to pay them off. Revenue bonds, on the other hand, must be paid off from revenue generated by the facility, and no property tax may be levied to make up any deficits. Second, the

Council also has established very detailed financial and reporting requirements for the operation of the facility. The proposed project will not be licensed unless the operator convinces the Council that the resale of its products will generate a profit capable of paying off the revenue bonds and covering all the anticipated operational costs. Whether these public resource-recovery plants will indeed be able to run at a profit remains to be seen. But the Council is at least trying to establish the groundwork to accomplish that goal.

Hazardous Waste Management

A special solid-waste problem is posed by the production of dangerous chemicals, radioactive materials, and other toxic matter within the metropolitan area. Hospitals regularly produce radioactive wastes that must be disposed of. Industries such as Minnesota Mining and Manufacturing produce dangerous chemical wastes that also must be accounted for. Until recently, little attention was paid to this problem. Chemical wastes were commonly dumped into sewer systems throughout the nation at no extra cost to the companies concerned. Local municipalities, dependent on a plant for an economic base, were in a poor position to regulate the dumpings. Metropolitan sewerage systems such as that of the MWCC, however, were less dependent on such plants. And after the enactment of state and federal water-quality standards, the metropolitan sewer boards were no longer allowed to discharge hazardous materials into the waterways. Thus pressures increased to make individual companies find ways to reuse such material or to find safe ways of storing them.

The MWCC's treatment plants cannot process chemical and hazardous wastes, and the MWCC has prohibited discharging them into the area's sewer system. Since not all these wastes can be recycled or reused by their producers, a substantial stock of hazardous waste is accumulating. To cope with this problem, the MWCC is attempting to identify all chemical and hazardous wastes that might be discharged into the metropolitan disposal system.[9] The federal Environmental Protection Agency has given Minnesota a 5 million dollar demonstration grant to design, construct, and operate an on-land disposal facility to handle chemical and hazardous waste produced within the state.[10] The MWCC will be the operating agency to carry out this grant.

Although still at the design stage, the MWCC's main problem in developing the plant has been to find a community willing to serve as the site for the facility. Nobody wants it in their neighborhood. The MWCC hopes to deal with this reluctance by starting with the identification of objective criteria for the facility and then searching for a number of optional sites that fit the criteria.

Water-Resource Policies

The Metropolitan Council's policies on water resources were adopted in 1973 to meet HUD requirements for including water-resource elements in the metropolitan comprehensive plan.[11] The Council's policies focus on three aspects of water-resource management: (1) ensuring adequate water supplies over the balance of the twentieth century, (2) ensuring that the quality of the water meets standards established by the MPCA and the 1972 Water Pollution Control Act and (3) protecting the hydrologic system.

Unlike many other urbanizing areas of the United States, the Twin Cities region has been blessed with an abundant water supply. Not only are there hundreds of lakes and three major rivers within the seven-county region, but the region sits on a mammoth ground-water aquifer. About half the water used comes from surface water and the other half from groundwater.[12] The major problem is that surface-water usage has been increasing at almost double the rate of population increase.[13] This has meant an increasing reliance on groundwaters. Although enough surface water exists to meet projected *average* needs until the end of the century, there will not be enough water to meet peak needs when the region experiences its next major drought similar to that of the 1930s.

Because there is the possibility of water shortages by the year 2000, the Metropolitan Council, the State Department of Natural Resources, and the United States Army Corps of Engineers are studying contingency plans to ensure adequate provisions. One critical problem is having enough reserves to augment the flow of the Mississippi River during low water-level periods. Since both Minneapolis and St. Paul draw their water from the Mississippi, the river must be kept at high enough levels to protect the city's water supply and quality. To ensure all communities a reasonable supply of water through the balance of the twentieth century, a set of effective water-resource policies must be established soon. The Council aims to update its water resources chapter in the *Development Guide* by 1981.

In seeking to improve the quality of water, many pollution problems from septic-tank failures have been corrected by the extension of the metropolitan sewer system.[14] Although this source of pollution has been dealt with, an additional threat is posed by surface-water runoff. This problem is addressed by a number of *Development Guide* chapters, including those on sanitary sewers, open space protection, and water resources, and a further revision of the water resources chapter is planned. The Council has been designated the Water Quality Management Agency under Section 208 of the federal 1972 Water Pollution Control Act. Section 208 addressed itself to nonpoint pollution, that is, pollution that enters the waterways from diffuse sources, such as fertilizers, pesticides, or other chemicals caught in storm-water runoff. Additionally, hazardous wastes entering rivers either through spills or through flooding of storage facilities located along floodplains pose a pollution threat. Electrical power plants that discharge heated water into the Mississippi and St. Croix rivers are a source of thermal pollution. All these problems are currently being studied for the revision of the water resources management policies.

A special aspect of maintaining high water quality is protecting the hydrologic system. This system is composed of *water bodies* and *water courses* (such as lakes, ponds, rivers, streams, and creeks), *wetlands* (such as marshes or swamps), *groundwater recharge areas*, and *floodplains*.[15] The Council's policies on *water bodies* and *water courses* have two aims—to protect them as natural drainageways where appropriate and to ensure that they meet state standards for shoreland management and water quality. The Council has urged local governments to classify their water bodies and water courses according to Minnesota standards and to zone them for specific uses.

Swamps, bogs, marshes, and other wetlands are important to the hydrologic system because they can filter silt and organic matter from storm-water runoff. They can also serve as wildlife habitats. When such wetlands are filled and are used as sites for houses and shopping centers, the storm-water runoff must settle elsewhere. It usually floods basements and necessitates the construction of expensive storm sewers. Ramsey County estimates that the cost of providing such storm sewers may be two and a half times the cost of maintaining natural drainage ways.[16]

Groundwater recharge areas are land areas with a permeable soil which permits water to drain down to the groundwater aquifers. The groundwater supplies are threatened by extensive paving in the wrong areas, improperly located solid-waste disposal sites, fertilizer and road-salt runoffs, and leaks from sewers and other pipelines.[17] To protect these areas, the Council's policies call on local governments to map the major recharge areas and to protect them by appropriate zoning and subdivision regulations.

Floodplains are areas adjacent to watercourses that have a 1 percent chance of flooding each year. The Council's policies instruct local governments to identify floodplains within their jurisdiction and to prevent development from occurring in these areas.

Other Areas That Merit Protection

In addition to open space critical to the hydrologic system, Council policies have also identified other areas which have special characteristics that merit protection from development. These are primarily forests and woodlands, production lands, and lands containing unique or endangered plants and animals. Protecting wooded areas is deemed important because such areas guard against soil erosion, are potential recreation areas, serve as agents in air purification, and can act as buffers against noise. Thus, Council policies call for incorporating wooded areas into local government development plans and encouraging subdivision regulations and development plans that avoid indiscriminate tree removal.

Two kinds of production areas are found within the metropolitan region. Prime agricultural land exists throughout much of the southern and western portions of the metropolis. Valuable mineral deposits such as sand, gravel, limestone, peat, and clay are found throughout the region. As discussed in Chapter 4, Council policies discourage converting agricultural lands to urban development. Concerning mineral production, the Council policies indicate that local comprehensive plans should provide performance standards for mining operations, reclamation, and reforestation. Finally, Council policies call for public purchasing of lands that contain unique or endangered plant or animal life and prohibiting developments that adversely affect them.

Implementing the Environmental Protection Policies

The implementation process for solid-waste disposal relies heavily on the counties, which are obliged to develop solid-waste master plans. These are then reviewed by the Metropolitan Council to see if they are consistent with the *Development Guide* chapter on solid waste. If they are not, the county and the Council must consult and resolve the differences. The implementation process for curbing point-source pollution of the water supply is being implemented primarily through the sewer plan discussed in Chapter 4.

Although an orderly and workable process has been achieved for implementing the sewers and solid-waste policies of the Council, the same cannot be said for water-resource policies. A serious problem is the fact that the lines of authority are not as clearly specified as in the other physical-policy areas. The Metropolitan Council has been designated the federal "208" agency to set water-resource policies; but more than forty federal, state, and local agencies particpate in planning, regulating, or managing water resources, including the MPCA, the Minnesota Departments of Health and Natural Resources, watershed districts, the United States Geological Survey, municipalities, counties, and the United States Army Corps of Engineers. Metropolitan Council planner Marcel R. Jouseau wrote that water-resource management "is performed in a piecemeal fashion by agencies at the federal, state and local levels. The state laws divide the responsibility for the management of the water resources among several agencies."[18]

Except for using its A-95 review powers, the Council's implementation of its water-resource policies has been limited to advisory and advocacy actions. It has produced maps that identify the areas requiring protection, so that local governments that have zoning responsibilities can match development proposals against open-space protection needs. The Council also provides considerable technical assistance to local governments on these questions. Specifically, it has provided local governments with a set of model ordinances that deal with environmental site planning, environmental overlay districts, conservation districts, mineral extraction, and agricultural preservation.[19] It has begun work on an *Environmental Protection Planning Handbook* similar to the *Agricultural Planning Handbook* provided local governments in 1976.[20] Finally, the Council played a key advocacy role in getting the Mississippi River Valley designated as a critical area.

In sum, however, the water-resources policies (other than those related to sewers) have not been implemented very well. The Council seems to be looking foward to the planning process established in 1976 as its major implementation tool in this area.

Social Policies

When the staff of the Metropolitan Planning Commission began to grapple with the physical development of the Twin Cities region in the 1950s, it was aware of the many social stresses that result from rapid suburban growth. Further, it was obvious that the plans for roads, sewers, and open space had many implications for the social quality of life. However, the planning profession was then very much oriented to the physical systems and land-use patterns of urban areas. It had not developed the techniques or the sense of urgency to give systematic attention to the ways in which these physical systems affected social relations. As it happened, these social-policy questions were dealt with indirectly and often quite casually by the technical decisions of planners concerned with physical development. It was hoped that if urban sprawl were slowed, sewers built as needed, and highways extended, better health, housing, and economic opportunities would follow. But no serious research was done to make sure that the "cause" in fact led to the desired "effect."

During the 1970s, the Metropolitan Council has incrementally entered the social-policy field. Although it is far from grasping the full interplay between physical and social-planning relationships, it is actively researching them. The main impetus for the Council's movement in this direction was not the inherent need for such attention, but the concern of the federal government to raise nationwide standards in certain social-policy areas. In most of the areas to be discussed here, a federal grant or planning mandate sparked

the Council's programs. This is not to say that the Council was reluctant, for in most cases its members and staff were very concerned.
But staff resources can be allocated to problems only if there is
enough money available to support such a commitment.

Housing Policy

The multi-headed problem of housing faces every urban area. Its
roots are in several common conditions and trends which, when
taken together, make it very difficult and expensive to attack. In
one form, the problem is the very limited housing choice for lower-
income households, especially outside the central-city neighborhoods. This is in large part as a result of the free-market economy
which segregates the lowest-cost dwellings into the least desirable
areas. It is also, for persons of racial and cultural minority groups,
the fruit of discrimination by white landowners and realtors in spite
of an array of laws to the contrary.

A second manifestation of the housing problem is the high and
steadily rising cost of new homes. The median price of a new home
now exceeds $50,000,[21] a figure that is beyond the means of more
than two-thirds of all households (allowing 25 percent of income
for shelter). This price has been rising approximately 1 percent each
month since 1971. Many factors cause this inflation—the cost of
land, labor, and materials, increased buyer demands for "extras,"
and governmental regulations on lot and home sizes and standards.[22]

The third aspect of the problem is the deterioration of existing
buildings and of the neighborhoods. Many structurally sound buildings, which could still house families for many years at relatively
low cost, are being lost owing to lack of maintenance and to being
located in areas made undesirable by decay and crime. Money for
rehabilitation is scarce because of the low income of residents and
the reluctance of lending institutions to finance the work. The magnitude of this task is illustrated by a recent survey taken by the
Council which determined that more than half of all dwelling units
in Minneapolis and St. Paul needed some rehabilitation.[23]

The Metropolitan Council's involvement in housing originated
in a 1966 policy statement of the Metropolitan Planning Commission aimed at securing a wide choice in residential location for all
persons, regardless of race, ethnic origin, or income. No means of

implementation accompanied this proposal, though. In 1967, the U.S. Department of Housing and Urban Development selected the Twin Cities area as one of three to receive a $100,000 grant to study metropolitan housing planning. Although its staff completed the report in 1969, the Council as a whole was reluctant to embark on a venture involving such a controversial social issue. Nevertheless, the staff continued its work and in 1971 secured adoption of the first housing-policy chapter. That document was significant in committing the Council for the first time to the basic goal of distributing lower-income housing throughout the region and to using its A-95 powers to back it up. Essentially, it put the cities on notice that when it reviewed their applications for federal grants for parks, sewers, and water facilities, and any others on which it could comment, it would give highest priority to those that were conforming to these housing goals. The public debates before and after the policy's adoption also helped build a political constituency on the issue, with the Greater Metropolitan Federation supporting the Council and many suburban governmental officials opposing the housing policy.

A revised plan issued in 1973 contained more criteria to guide Council housing decisions and set forth a more detailed implementation program. By this time the Council had also acquired the direct power to review requests for federal housing grants. Experience with that plan led to the 1977 revision which sets numerical goals for subsidized dwelling units in each city. The new plan also covers the distribution of funds for home rehabilitation and for middle-income mortgages. Essentially, it is a major step toward a comprehensive plan for allocating all public investments in the region's housing.

The core of the Metropolitan Council's current program is the Fair Share plan for distributing subsidized housing for low-income families and elderly persons. The cities of Minneapolis and St. Paul are allotted 30 percent of the units which can be built with federal funds that the area anticipates receiving in the near future. The inner suburbs (such as Edina, Roseville, and South St. Paul) will draw most of the remainder. A city's share is calculated by a formula that considers its number of households and jobs, the anticipated growth in each by 1990, and the number of low-income households not currently living in subsidized housing. Of this figure, at least 60 percent of the units must be for families rather than the elderly, who have been the prime beneficiaries of such housing in the past. Further, a given city may have high or low priority for subsidized housing funds, depending on its proximity to the two central business districts, other employment centers, transit and shopping facilities.[24]

The "teeth" in this policy are the Council's powers over the flow of federal funds, as it demonstrated to Golden Valley in 1971, to give one example. Each city in the region that has applied for grants under the 1974 Housing and Community development Act had to prepare a three-year plan to meet housing needs of lower-income persons. The Metropolitan Council reviewed each application to recommend initial funding (and all were approved). The Council is using the Fair Share plan as a general basis for evaluation and will probably be satisfied with fulfillment of two-thirds of a city's goal after the three-period. As of mid-1977 this fund cutoff power had not been used, although twelve Hennepin County suburbs had been warned to move faster. Although the Council judges these specific goals to be important spurs to housing progress, it has also spent much time assisting and negotiating with these cities' officials and is the channel for financial aid as well.

Acting as the Metropolitan Housing and Redevelopment Authority (MHRA), the Council allocates funds under Section 8 of the Housing and Community Development Act of 1974 for rent supplements for low-income households. These homes remain in private ownership and are located on scattered sites to avoid becoming "ghettos." Such housing units, leased for ths purpose, can be used to fulfill the community's housing plan. The Council as HRA also administers a rehabilitation grant program in sixty-two suburbs with money from the Minnesota Housing Finance Agency. Rehabilitation is politically more popular than subsidized housing since it encourages neighborhood stability. The MHRA also helps cities administer their programs and in accounting, publicity, and staff training.

The Council has also begun to attack the new-home-cost problem. A section of the 1976 Metropolitan Land Planning Act directed it to research all the contributing factors and make recommendations for cost savings, with particular attention to local land and building codes and ordinances. Subsequently, the Council and the Association of Metropolitan Municipalities joined forces to survey those municipal regulations. In June 1977 they agreed on a set of minimum standards for house and lot size that were suggested to the cities as a way to lower home costs. A recent study by a major residential developer showed that savings of more than 10 percent could be realized from Bloomington's reduction of its minimum standards.[25] The Council also initiated, in summer 1977, an annual competition among designers and builders to produce desirable modest-cost homes as a way of gaining publicity for this program.

There is evidence that the Department of Housing and Urban Development will in the near future take more seriously its professed ideal of ending racial and income segregation in housing. It has begun to withhold Community Development funds from cities that have not made adequate effort. The Metropolitan Council's housing policy is now one of the most progressive in the nation, and it anticipates stronger federal support for its enforcement efforts. In the past, the Department of Housing and Urban Development and the Minnesota Housing Finance Agency have not always conformed to the Council's plan in distributing their funds. At the same time, there are many complex social and economic conditions that can be only indirectly affected by government, and then with much political and technical difficulty. Regional authorities can work with such problems as home location, but most cost factors are susceptible only to national action.

Health Policy

At first glance, the health status of people in the Twin Cities area is quite good, relative to the rest of the nation. The infant mortality rate, a common indicator of the quality of overall medical care, was 7.4 per 1,000 births, just over half that of the United States as a whole.[26] Further, the region has many more than the national average of physicians, hospitals, nursing homes, and public-health programs. Nevertheless, two broad problems are shared with the rest of the country. The first is the cost of medical care, rising faster than the purchasing power of the average household. By 1976, health costs made up 8.6 percent of the gross national product, up from 5.9 percent in 1965.[27] Among the factors causing this rise has been the heavy investment in hospitals and their increasingly sophisticated equipment and specialized services. The second problem is that neither good health nor health services are evenly distributed throughout the population. The poor, the elderly, and the racial and cultural minorities have not had the access to health care enjoyed by most others, even in the cities where it is usually no more than a few blocks from their home.

The Metropolitan Council embarked upon health planning under both state and federal directives. In 1970, it was given its initial responsibilities under the Comprehensive Health Planning Act which Congress passed in 1966. In 1976, this role was strengthened when it was provisionally designated as a Health Systems Agency as required by the National Health Planning and Resources Development Act of 1974. The state-granted powers are based on the 1971 Certificate of Need law. Before any health-care facility in the state can expand its plant or services, it must obtain a state certificate showing that the expansion is needed. A provider in the Twin Cities region must first apply for this through the Metropolitan Council.

Both levels of government also mandated a set of plans and policies to coordinate the region's health care. The current statement of these is the Health Systems Plan for the metropolitan area, adopted by the Council in 1977 and required by federal legislation to be amended yearly. It lists eight broad goals or directions for policy:

(1) Improve the overall health . . . by promoting projects that will have beneficial effects on the health of the population.
(2) Study the status of the health of the people . . . in order to make the appropriate decision about what health services are needed and where they are needed most.
(3) Make people aware of their rights and responsibilities regarding their own health and the health of their neighbors.
(4) Encouraging . . . innovations that show promise of improving the health of the people without increasing the cost of health care overall.
(5) Keep the cost of health services at a reasonable level.
(6) Include providers of health services in the planning process.
(7) Encourage health-care institutions to share services and . . . coordinate them in a network that makes the most efficient use of the most expensive services.
(8) Establish a defined but flexible system of health services, organized into a service network.[28]

This list is followed by fifty-eight policies that embody these goals in the form of priorities and responsibilities. They emphasize, for example, preventive health care, primary services for medically underserved people, use of existing facilities to meet new needs as far as possible, and involvement of local and neighborhood organizations that reflect particular cultures and concerns. The plan then continues with a lengthy description of specific service systems for ten forms of care, from perinatal service to chemical dependency programs.

The key agency for preparing and implementing these policies is the Metropolitan Health Board (MHB). Although classified as an advisory committee, its existence is based on state and federal law, and it performs some unique functions. It has twenty-nine members appointed by the Council for staggered terms of three years. One is chosen from each of the sixteen Council districts, and the other thirteen are selected at large; all seven counties must have at least one representative. Federal guidelines stipulate that at least sixteen of the members must be consumers of health services as distinguished from providers (e.g., doctors, hospital administrators, medical-school faculty, and nursing-home owners). The MHB staff serves at the pleasure of the board rather than under the Metropolitan Council. Since the MHB's budget is derived largely from federal grants, the Council exercises only review, not approval, authority over its finances.

Actual delivery of health care is very decentralized, each county having its own public-health agency. Most services are provided by private physicians and other practitioners in business for themselves. The MHB's task is to get these decentralized providers of health-care services to adhere to the policies stated in the Health Systems Plan. It has four basic tools to do this.

First, the MHB must develop an annual implementation plan that indicates how it will carry out the overall objectives of the *Health Guide* for the coming year.

Second, it makes recommendations for certificates of need in the seven-county region. When the Metropolitan Council receives such a request, the MHB reviews and holds hearings on it to learn whether the stated need could be met without that expansion. It passes its recommendation on to the Metropolitan Council, and noncontro-

versial requests are ratified without much discussion. But controversial issues are discussed first in the Council's Human Resources
Committee and are often sent back to the MHB for futher consideration. For example, in March 1977 the committee remanded a recommendation for a brain scanner on the grounds that more study was
needed regarding the possibility that several hospitals could share
the device. To date, the Metropolitan Council and the MHB have
been able to work out all differences and send a joint recommendation to the State Board of Health which gives final approval. If
they were to have an irreconcilable disagreement, the state board
would have to choose between the two recommendations.

A third tool of the MHB is the power to review and approve all
federal grants for public health, drug abuse, and mental-health programs. By mid-1977, the MHB can only make recommendations to
the Metropolitan Council for exercising its A-95 review and comment powers on these grants. Once the MHB is fully certified as the
region's health-systems agency, it will be the final authority for review of these requests. Under the present review-and-comment arrangement, the U.S. Department of Health, Education and Welfare
sometimes fails to support the Metropolitan Council's recommendations. When the MHB has final authority on grant allocation, federal
agencies will be obliged to support the MHB's decision.[29]

Finally, once it is fully certified, the MHB will also receive authority to review the appropriateness of existing services. Certificates of need and A-95 reviews apply only to new facilities and do
not concern existing ones. Under its new powers, the MHB will be
able to determine, for example, that a particular hospital should
not have a pediatrics department or perhaps that three hospitals
should share prenatal facilities. It can also support these judgments
with the awarding of grants, of course. These reviews of appropriateness are expected to be influential with the public and with practicing medical personnel. It is hoped that pediatricians would avoid
sending patients to a hospital whose pediatrics facilities have been
judged inappropriate by the MHB. In fall 1977, a major effort in
hospital planning was begun in response to directives issued by the
U.S. Department of Health, Education and Welfare to bring the number of available beds and related facilities in line with current needs.
The excess capacity that now exists contributes to the inflation in

medical-care costs, and a broad-range federal program is being as-sembled to bring some of these costs under tighter control.

The implementation process for the MHB health policies has evolved over the past half decade, and its newest tools are as yet un-tested. The metropolitan Health Systems Plan has set some laudable and far-reaching goals whose attainment would surely be beneficial to the metropolitan area. Whether the implementation process is commensurate with the goals will be of vital concern to all providers and consumers of health care and will be closely monitored by the Metropolitan Council in the coming years.

Policies for the Aging

In 1970, 9 percent of the metropolitan area's people, about 163,000, were sixty-five or older. Most lived in Minneapolis or St. Paul. Ninety-two percent lived alone or with families or friends rather than in institutions such as nursing homes. Of these senior citizens, about 20 percent were living on incomes below the poverty level, and nearly half suffered from a chronic health problem.[30] Clearly, any public policy that aims to ensure some minimum level of care for these persons must be both far-ranging and sensitive to individual needs.

Like its housing efforts, the Metropolitan Council's aging program sprang from federal initiatives. In 1965, Congress passed the Older Americans Act and established the Administration on Aging within the Department of Health, Education and Welfare. Its purpose was to strengthen local public and private services to the elderly. Amend-ments to that act in 1971 required substate regional planning for such services, and in the next year the Minnesota Governor's Citi-zens Council on Aging designated the Metropolitan Council the area planning agency. The latter was then provided with a grant to begin planning, and it created a twenty-five-member advisory committee to supply citizen assistance and viewpoints. Each year the Council submits its funding plan to the Governor's Citizens Council, which must approve it before it can be carried out.

The Administration on Aging has set out certain goals and direc-tives for the area agencies. First, they must study the needs for social services, such as medical care, housing, and transportation, among their own aged populations and coordinate a system to meet them.

Second, they are to see that information about these services reaches all elderly persons so they can take advantage of them. Finally, there are to be regular evaluations of each program, taking into account the views and experiences of the elderly themselves. These agencies are also to be alert to the impact of special crises on the elderly, such as the recent jumps in fuel costs, and work to prevent or alleviate hardships.

The Metropolitan Council's aging program has two additional objectives, centering on maximizing independence and opportunities for older persons with appropriate services and facilities. To achieve these requires a combination of public and private resources, channeled through new programs or expansion of existing ones. The goal of in-home independence could be served by providing meals and housekeeping services and improved transportation, for example. In essence, the Council seeks to link all elderly persons in the region, especially those who live away from the mainstream of urban life, with any sources of help they may need.

To carry out these objectives costs money, and the Metropolitan Council must thus serve as a link between the service agencies and the fund sources. In 1976, the Council processed twenty-eight applications from both private and governmental sources to the Administration on Aging and commented favorably on all but one. In that year, it distributed about $450,000 to support fifteen programs in such areas as health, legal aid, transportation, and in-home services.[31] As a guide in assessing these requests, the Council must set out its priorities, usually meeting urgent needs for which no organized action is currently taken. From these, a comprehensive area plan for the aging is gradually developing. It will necessarily be a broad one, since much of the Council's planning concerns the elderly in some fashion. For example, members of the Aging Advisory Committee have joined with the Criminal Justice Advisory Committee to study crime against the elderly.

Since the Council's efforts in this area are indirect, it is not easy to identify their impact. However, many of the programs begun with funds it allocated are now continuing with support from regional sources. It has also directed considerable publicity toward the problems of the aging. It must conduct public meetings on the adoption of each year's funding priorities, and some modifications have resulted from them. The surveys and advisory committee activities have also increased citizen influence to some extent. The data that have been collected are a resource ready to be used by the service agencies to improve their own efforts. However, participation by minority and low-income aged remains minimal, and their special needs are perhaps still being overlooked.

Criminal Justice Policies

The administration of criminal justice at state and local levels in the United States could well be described as a "nonsystem." That is, there are several different components, such as the police, the courts, and the correctional institutions, working without adequate communication with one another and often at cross-purposes. This label of nonsystem certainly applies to the Twin Cities area, with its many municipal police departments, county sheriff's offices, jails, detention centers, workhouses, county and municipal courts, and the entire state law enforcement and corrections processes. The Metropolitan Council and many of the criminal justice personnel have recognized the need to draw these units closer together in pursuit of common objectives, though not necessarily by organizational consolidation.

The Metropolitan Council entered the field of criminal justice when, after passage by Congress of the Omnibus Crime Control and Safe Streets Act of 1968, it was designated the criminal-justice planning unit for the metropolitan area. In that role, it was to review local government applications for funds from the Law Enforcement Assistance Administration (LEAA) of the U.S. Department of Justice for their crime control programs. In 1970, the Council appointed a thirty-three-member advisory committee which, together with its staff, began to prepare a comprehensive criminal-justice plan.

The law and justice chapter of the *Development Guide* was adopted in 1973. Its primary purpose was to state priorities and criteria to be followed in evaluating the grant applications. For example, it recommended that technical support services to police and sheriffs' departments, such as communications and crime laboratories, be centralized to operate more efficiently. Thus a request for funds to establish a single county crime lab would have a good chance of being approved. High priority was also given to community-based corrections, reform of treatment of juveniles with minor offenses, and increased resources for rehabilitation of adult offenders. In that plan, the Council also made numerous recommendations for new legislation at the state level. For example, it urged that the offender rehabilitation process be decentralized to the community level as much as possible, and the Legislature responded a year later with the Community Corrections Act.

Current efforts of the Council fall into three categories. First, the review of grant applications continues. In response to the Council's priorities, many of the proposed programs are oriented to youth or are focused on the specific justice needs of neighborhoods.

Second, the policy plan is soon to be revised to reflect shifting regional goals and to advance beyond those stated in 1973. Recent Congressional legislation mandated regional and state crime control planning as a condition to receiving LEAA grants. The Metropolitan Council is the designated regional planner, in cooperation with the state's newly established Crime Control Planning Board. Upon the initiative of the Criminal Justice Advisory Committee, planning has also begun for the reduction of juvenile crime and to interrelate the many juvenile justice agencies now operating.

Finally, the Council staff has worked with local governments in a variety of assistance efforts. It has laid the groundwork for establishing a single emergency telephone number (911) for the metropolitan area. This was a complex task, involving police, fire, and ambulance services in over 200 political jurisdictions, plus the region's six telephone companies. Once in operation, it will enable a person to dial 911 for any emergency and be automatically connected with the agency responsible for the area in which the telephone is located. In another case, it gave staff time and funds to help consolidate investigation and communciations operations in the sheriffs' offices in Anoka and Washington counties. Finally, at the request of forty-four suburban police departments, it made a study of police hiring standards. This was made necessary by recent federal laws invalidating all standards, for example, height and physical strength, that are not directly related to job performance.

In the future, there is likely to be greater emphasis on public safety, the "other side" of the criminal-justice coin, and attention to its relevance to all Council policies. For example, safety and crime prevention are important components in housing, transportation, and youth employment programs. This will call for some reshaping of the current law and justice policies and reordering of some of its priorities.

Communications Policy

Communications is not a "problem area" as are those to which the previous policies are directed. It is more oriented to potential than to current needs, and so has not been as high on the Council's priority list. The Metropolitan Council entered this field in 1971 through a narrow door: cable television. In a legal dispute over the award of a cable franchise by the city of Bloomington, the Council was asked to rule whether that action had "metropolitan significance." Lacking a basis for deciding, the Council could not comment, and the court ruled in favor of the city. However, the Council formed an advisory committee on cable communications, which recommended, late in 1972, state legislation to govern cable systems and Council actions to provide for the interconnection of metropolitan area service. The Legislature responded in 1973 with a comprehensive Cable Communications Act that, among other things, gave the Metropolitan Council a planning role and the right to be consulted by the state in administering the law.

By 1974 the Council had completed studies on districting the region to group adjacent cities for shared cable franchises and on interconnecting the district systems to provide some area-wide programming. Late in 1975 it changed the name of its advisory committee to Communications, to register its desire that the field be viewed more broadly. The original Metropolitan Council Act called for public library planning, and the A-95 review requirements cover post office construction and federal grants for local libraries. In addition there are communications-related concerns in policies for criminal justice, health, and transportation.

As a step toward a general policy plan, a Communications Service Objectives Report, issued in 1976, proposed eight goals and nine policies for study. The first and most basic goal was that every person in the region have access to information adequate for survival and personal development. One means of fulfilling it, according to the report, is to set up an emergency communications service adequate to each person's security. A typical policy statement advocated efforts to make communication resources available to the most disadvantaged groups in society. This may necessitate some kind of free hookup to a cable that reaches all homes. In the near future, the progress that is likely to be made will touch specific problems, such as expanding cable television and pricing telephone service. Yet, the policy chapter that will emerge must provide an overall set of goals and priorities within which the many options can be assessed.

Promotion of the Arts

An increasing number of citizens are concerned that the fine and performing arts be recognized as essential to the quality of life. Minnesota has had a State Arts Board since 1966 which has granted funds for local and regional arts projects. In 1976 that board assigned to the Metropolitan Council the responsibility for the Twin Cities area to assess arts needs and develop a plan for meeting them. The Council in turn established a Regional Arts Task Force, made up of its own members plus eight citizens who are involved in the arts. In early 1977, work began on this assignment, aimed at formulating a proposal to the State Arts Board for a block grant that would aid selected arts activities in the region. The basic goals are to increase the visibility of arts activities and make them accessible to all citizens, raise the level of artistic achievement, foster a stable working environment for artists, and promote cooperation and resource sharing among them.

Toward a Social Development Framework

All these social policies, seen as individual functions, lack an inherent common denominator. The Council entered each social field separately, in response to different needs and to federal and state programs which were themselves quite disparate. Council personnel and advisory committees are identified with their functions and had no special mandate until very recently to cooperate with one another. However, it is now clearly recognized that each social policy has implications for all the others and that it is essential to relate all of them to a general development framework.

A second issue is the fact that "social policy" in the Twin Cities area is much broader than these few function that the Metropolitan

Council is concerned with. By one estimate, there are about 2,500 public and private agencies that provide social services, from family assistance and drug counseling to employment referrals and aid to the handicapped. With so many, it is inevitable that there is overlap and duplication of services, with reduced results per dollar spent, as well as failure to serve others who need it. Several agencies may compete with one another for funds and clienteles, and work at cross-purposes.

Third, an enormous sum of money is spent each year on social services in the region. This encompasses the funds spend directly by local, state, and national governments, those raised and spent by private institutions, and those from governmental sources that are passed through private agencies (as in medical care). Amounts in all three categories have risen steadily and no slacking off is likely. But these investment decisions are made piecemeal by many persons and groups, and there is no set of priorities for meeting the most pressing needs.

The Council chose to give first priority to integrating its physical development policies, as has been described. But in 1975, it secured a grant from the Department of Health, Education and Welfare—$80,000 for the first year and $100,000 for the second—to support work on a Social Development Framework that would complement the physical plan. Beginning in 1975, the staff and advisory committees in the human resources area, and the Council Human Resources Committee, have been studying the social impacts of physical and economic development, surveying the financing and outcomes of public and private social-service programs, and assembling a goals/policies plan which will link these separate functions.

Because human beings have much more complex and subtle existences in their social relationships than in their physical environments, planners find it harder to describe them in useful terms. It has become necessary for the Council to think of society as an intricate human ecology system with many interlocking units, such as the economic, political, educational, and familial. Any event or action—whether by government or a private source—that is directed at one unit will probably impact on the others as well. For example, a program to create jobs for unemployed youth can have a "ripple effect" on schools, the crime rate, and minority-group politics.

The initial efforts of the Social Framework staff have focused on improving the capacity of the metropolitan area to make decisions on social policy. This involves several steps. First, there must be a statement of overall goals and policies that bridge the gaps between the specific functions. The second requirement is for a set of social indicators that measure in some approximate way how the region stands with respect to these goals. Third, the priorities for financial investments in social services and facilities need to be decided, as criteria for allocating funds. Next, there have to be standards for measuring the impacts and outcomes of the many social programs. The fifth step involves recommendations to governmental policy makers at all levels about their roles in the human service system and those of the private sector. Last, there should be devised a regular means for involving ordinary citizens in this whole process, including a representative share of the poor and others who would not normally participate.

For those who are understandably concerned about the potential for bureaucratic tyranny and rigidity in this plan, the Council staff answers that big government, big business, and big social institutions all wield much power over people's lives. If average citizens are to harness or counter those power centers in their own interest, there will have to be an understandable means of planning and coordination that they can take part in. The hope is to see social needs met as much as possible within the smaller neighborhoods and communities by institutions that are "at home" there. This may take the form of grass-roots organizations serving the multiple needs of the elderly in that neighborhood, for example, or of the handicapped. But this requires that the community identify itself as such and learn how to make its own social-policy decisions. The Council cannot bring this about by fiat, nor can any law create a viable citizen-participation process. All that can be done by higher levels of government is to allow the local groups to take those initiatives and to support them as necessary with money, information, and coordination of the regional agencies that operate among them.

CHAPTER 6

Evaluation and Prospects

For over a decade the system of metropolitan governance in the Twin Cities has steadily evolved. The Metropolitan Council was created in 1967 as a unique regional institution — neither a general-purpose government nor just a COG. As it faced a series of successive crises and bitter political conflicts over sewers, airports, transit, and land use, its powers were increased by the Minnesota Legislature. It used this growing authority to establish metropolitan-level policies for a wide variety of public problems. And to carry out these policies, it has been given an impressive array of implementation tools.

What has all this activity for the past decade amounted to? Is it mostly symbolic sound and fury that signifies nothing? Or is the Minnesota system of metropolitan governance truly coping with suburban sprawl, rejuvenating the fully developed areas, coordinating the metropolitan special districts, alleviating social inequities, and accomplishing all its other *Development Guide* goals to improve the quality of life for its citizens? In short, how is one to evaluate and assess the system's performance to date?

This chapter approaches the question of evaluation from five perspectives. What outcomes can reasonably be attributed to the new system of governance? How effective is the Development Framework? What trends seem likely for the continued evolution

112

of the Council's role? What major current issues remain unresolved? And is the Minnesota approach transferable?

Outcomes

What has the Metropolitan Council accomplished during its history? This question is hard to answer precisely for several reasons. First, it operates within a complex of governments—national, state, regional, and local. The concept of "marble cake federalism" discussed in Chapter 4 portrays a sharing of policy-making responsibility between them but also suggests why credit or blame is so hard to assign. As a policy maker, the Council has received directives and authority not only from the Minnesota Legislature which has direct legal control over it, but also from state administrative agencies, Congress, and federal agencies.

The panorama of policy implementation is even more complex. For implementing some policies, such as its highway plans, the Council depends on federal and state agencies, as sources of grants or of compliance. To accomplish many other policies, the Council must secure the compliance of the other 272 governmental units in the metropolitan area, over which it has varying amounts of authority. Finally, there is a host of private organizations, such as hospitals, housing developers, and social-service agencies, whose activities relate to Council policies. Thus, there are probably no "pure" Council achievements or failures.

A second difficulty in assessing the Council's impact is the dynamic nature of the metropolitan community. To ask how the metropolitan area would be different today had a voluntary council of governments been established instead of the Metropolitan Council is futile, for some policies would most likely have appeared in any case. There certainly would have been action on sewage disposal, transportation, parks, and health, although they may well have been different from the present policies. The region would have devised alternate ways to govern itself, but the authors believe these alternatives would most likely have been less effective than the present Council. In this respect also, Council achievements and shortcomings are hard to isolate from the general currents of development.

Despite these reservations, the system of metropolitan governance established since 1967 has produced a number of important outcomes. First, and perhaps most fundamental, the Metropolitan Council has achieved considerable legitimacy and respect as an institution. Second, its metropolitan policies have begun to make a noticeable impact on the life of the region. And third, a regional political process has begun to emerge.

Legitimacy

Even though specific actors disagree with specific policies or fear future growth of its powers, the need for the Metropolitan Council is no longer questioned. Other governing officials appear to view the Council with respect. This is perhaps clearest with its parent authority, the Legislature. The incremental expansion of its responsibilities by the lawmakers illustrates this well. They constantly chose to focus metropolitan policy-making authority in the Council and let it make the effort to interrelate the disparate functions.

Among local government officials, this status of legitimacy is slightly weaker. In general public officials from the fully developed area view the Council much more favorably than do officials from the outlying suburbs. In spring 1976, the League of Women Voters surveyed the attitudes of local elected and staff officials toward the Metropolitan Council, conducting eighty-one interviews in thirty-four communities.[1] Sixty-eight percent of the respondents indicated an overall satisfaction with the Council, and 32 percent expressed varying amounts of dissatisfaction. When asked how responsive the Council is to local governments, 74 percent answered "very" or "somewhat." In both issues, local administrative personnel were more positive toward the Council than were elected officials. Sixty-five percent of the respondents thought they had an adequate understanding of Council policies, and slightly more than half thought they had adequate means of influencing its decisions. Negative answers to the question on influence were centered heavily among elected officials and both elected and administrative persons from small suburbs and rural areas.

Although the survey found strong support for the Council generally, local officials do not support any significant increases in the Council's powers and financing. Nearly half of the respondents wanted its powers and finances held at the current level; a third favored reduction; and only a small minority suggested expansion. Elected local officials were much less supportive of expanding Council powers than were local appointed officials. The elected officials were evenly divided between reduction and holding powers at the current levels.

The executive director of the Association of Metropolitan Municipalities, Vern Peterson, reports that although there remains some distrust of the Council by local officials — some would even like to see it abolished — the general attitude supports a pragmatic cooperation with the Council in the hope of influencing its policies. Many agree that it is performing functions that the local units cannot perform on their own, but some officials feel that the Legislature has given it powers it does not need. In the areas of housing and land-use controls, joint efforts to work out standards and programs have increased greatly after passage of the Metropolitan Land Planning Act of 1976. The local units' relations with Chairman Boland have also been excellent, in that he views them as the Council's chief clientele and seeks to work by voluntary agreement rather than confrontation.[2]

Besides the local officials, strong support for the Council has been expressed by the Greater Metropolitan Federation, the League of Women Voters, the Citizens League, and the metropolitan daily newspapers. Many other political organizations have not given vocal support per se, but have come to deal with the Council as an established reality with significant power to act for their benefit or detriment. There are no significant groups campaigning either to abolish it or reduce its powers. Opposition that has developed in the distant and less urbanized suburbs is not united enough to conduct more than a delaying action in the Legislature.

Policy Impact

From the achievement of legitimacy, it is logical to turn to the policies and actions of the Metropolitan Council that are the bases for these judgments. In Chapters 4 and 5 we surveyed those policies and the means for implementing them. Yet, as indicated earlier in this chapter, most of the Council's policies are shared within a chain of partially responsible agencies — federal, state, and local. A plan to locate low-income housing within Edina, for example, is simultaneously a national, state, regional, and municipal policy. Within this network, the Council's impact is much stronger under some conditions than it is under others. Four conditions seem critical.

First, some of the Council's most important successes occurred when it served as a link between the general goals of national and state policies and their adoption on the local scene. In the case of housing, progress began to be made in distributing subsidized dwellings to reluctant suburban communities only when the Council used its A-95 review powers to back up that aim. Further, progress shifted from a slow to a moderate pace when the Council's fair share policy set explicit goals for each city. As a rule, its policies will have greater impact when this linkage is clear and well understood and when the higher agencies support the Council with funds and respect for its priorities and recommendations.

Second, the Council has had a significant impact when it could organize a function on a regional level that the local units could not perform for themselves in a systematic way. Waste management and mass transit are two obvious examples, for these have been adequately managed only since the Council attained policy control over their respective agencies through the Metropolitan Reorganization Act of 1974. Although unresolved questions remain and disputes still occur, there is no longer any doubt that the MWCC and the MTC are subordinate to the Council for planning and policy purposes. After a recent study of the Council's environmental management programs, Michael Gleeson concluded that "council policy has been reflected in final output to a remarkable extent. This is true of very general policy, as for example, the move from open dumps to sanitary landfills, and of quite specific policy, like the location of the landfills relative to neighboring land uses."[3]

Third, the Council's policy impact can be significant when its plans reflect the interests of the units that are to implement it, and impose few or no costs in return. The mechanism for channeling urban growth by drawing an Urban Service Line is controversial, to be sure, but many communities expect to benefit from it. A city that is located just "inside" that line and wants urban growth may gain more of that growth if urban sprawl is prohibited beyond it. On the other hand, a rural community close to urban centers that wants to exclude high-density development will want to remain "outside" the line. Of course, when a city finds itself on the "wrong side" of the line, it may protest. But the former situation seems more typical, and the MUSA line was mapped partially by such criteria. In such a case, the Development Framework has its best chance of being effective.

Finally, the Council can make effective policy if it can correlate plans and goals for many separate functions and avoid conflicts between them as they touch the local units. During the Council's first five years, it gave most of its attention to resolving local service crises and tooling up to respond to federal planning mandates in the separate functional areas. It realized the need for comprehensive planning that would integrate all these, but funds for that were lacking and the sense of urgency for it had not yet developed. As a result, city officials encountered many conflicts and contradictions between specific policies, and frustration with the Council became widespread.

The period since 1972, however, has seen the growth and emergence of a comprehensive growth plan for the region that encompasses the policies for waste management, transportation, and regional parks, and which is slowly incorporating action on housing and water resources as well. An assessment of the Development Framework is given later in this chapter. It is enough at this point to note that the very preparation of such a comprehensive plan is an achievement, for its linking of major physical systems policies is a precondition for effective growth management by the cities and counties.

To state the conditions that make the Council's policy making effective is to suggest that their absence or opposites hinder its achievement. Gleeson found that in reviewing municipal sanitary plans the Council had more difficulty working with the MPCA, over which it had no control, than it had working with the MWCC.[4] If the Council's role as a gateway in the federal-to-local flow of funds is bypassed when the U.S. Department of Health, Education and Welfare avoids the A-95 review in awarding grants, its social policies will be that much less effective.

It may be that a ten-year span is not long enough to evaluate some of the Council's plans and their outcomes. The Development Framework took eight years to prepare. Most social policies have been given a much lower priority, and they may be inherently harder to formulate owing to the extensive role of private organizations. In the coming two to five years, the Council faces a major challenge in integrating its many social policies with one another and with the *Development Guide*. If it can do this with growing success, then the individual policies also have a brighter prospect for effectiveness.

A Regional Political Process

Political activity takes place wherever there are public-policy decisions that carry important stakes for some people and groups. Thus, one talks about national, state, and city politics, meaning that there is at each point a set of authoritative decision makers who are surrounded by other actors seeking to influence their decisions. The Metropolitan Council has become the nucleus for such a political process, centered on the issues that concern the metropolitan region as a whole.

There are five aspects that should be studied in viewing the Council as a regional political arena. First, it could be argued that a "regional interest" can be identified that is distinct from the local interests of municipalities and the broader state and national interests of governments at those levels. When the entire region is affected by the way in which waste is managed, water supplied, transportation planned, and crime prevented, certain actors emerge who argue that these matters should not be left to the narrow perspectives of municipal and county governments. Only a regional constituency and process can grasp these on a large enough scale. At the same time, this regional public interest must be defended *vis-à-vis* the general standards and plans of state and national governments. A persistent criticism of federal administrative agencies in particular is that they ignore the unique characteristics and needs of the many local areas and are too ready to impose their uniform values on them.

To maintain an effective regional identity, the Metropolitan Council must be an advocate for the area as a whole, facing both "upward" and "downward" on the governmental ladder. The Development Framework and the emerging Social Framework define the regional, as distinct from the local, public values (but do not necessarily contradict them). As it defined standards for distributing subsidized housing through the region, the Council went well beyond the demands of the U.S. Department of Housing and Urban Development. But in doing so, the Council was able to claim bonus funds for rent subsidy purposes. The federal A-95 review process has opened a wide door of authority and resources to regional agencies that actually function as a decision-making arena and can assert their interest effectively.

A second and equally essential key to regional politics is the control over allocating resources. Many political scientists define politics as the "authoritative allocation of values,"[5] and all political conflict takes place, ultimately, over *who* allocates *what* to *whom*. The Metropolitan Council allocates many resources to many other actors. Most obvious is what it spends on its own operations—more than 5.2 million dollars in 1977. More important is the larger sum that passes to local public and private recipients in the form of federal and state grants upon the Council's direct award or favorable comment. Although the Council does not have sole authority over these, it shapes the final decision much more often than not. It also controls directly the capital investments that are made in sewers, transit, airports, and regional parks. Finally, the Council also expects to gain influence over large private investments through its new metropolitan significance rules and over county and municipal capital spending by means of its metropolitan investment policies. As it achieves this control, the Council will indeed be able to allocate authoritatively so many "valued things" as to be a potent political actor.

Third, an established regional political process will draw and nurture "regional politicians." Edward Knudson, then an outside consultant who studied the Council's comprehensive planning process in 1974-75, observed:

The structures of the Metropolitan Council have facilitated the development of a new kind of "regional politician." Urban growth policy was not just a technical or legal issue, but a political issue, demanding a political solution with strong political leadership. Since the regional politician enjoys regular interaction with professional planners, he or she becomes an informed political leader. The regional politician at the Metro Council can be concerned first with broad policy issues rather than the infinite details and crises of agencies and governments which actually own and operate physical facilities or systems.[6]

As Knudson later explained, this regional politician is one who thinks of the metropolitan area as a whole in defining his or her political knowledge and interests. These persons may be members of the Council itself, to the extent that they significantly transcend their own districts in their policy values. John Boland, the current chairman, and Robert Hoffman, former chairman of the Council's Physical Development Committee, have provided strong leadership in this regard. To name all the other regional politicians would be a formidable task, but they are found in state and local governments, civic organizations, and business.

Regional politicians also tend to create regional interest groups to represent their concerns. At the area-wide level, the cities within the seven-county area, long organized within the League of Minnesota Cities, formed a separate section in 1967, largely to lobby with the Metropolitan Council and the Legislature on metropolitan policy questions. The Metropolitan InterCounty Council was formed for the same purpose. As has already been described, the Citizens League had an instrumental role in the design and subsequent growth of the Council, and continues to regard it as the cornerstone of all regional policies. Clusters of groups also communicate with the Council on specific matters, from environmental protection to services for the elderly.

Fourth, to be a genuine political arena in a democratic political system, there must be channels for public accountability and citizen participation. The Metropolitan Council does not meet the first criterion fully, since it answers to the public only through the governor of Minnesota, who appoints it, and through the Legislature which has granted its powers. Later in this chapter, the arguments and prospects for a directly elected Council are examined. As for citizen participation, the sheer number of persons who sit on the permanent advisory committees is impressive — 563. Some committees, such as the Transportation Advisory Board, the Land Use Advisory Committee, and the Metropolitan Housing and Redevelopment Advisory Committee, make important inputs to policy, at least from the perspective of the local officials who belong to them.[7] Other are more peripherally involved with major decisions. Despite some shortcomings of this process it remains significant as a regularized structure for sources of advice, alternatives, and grievances that most other metropolitan areas lack. The Advisory Commission on Intergovernmental Relations concluded in a 1977 report that the Council's provisions for citizen participation are "probably the foremost in the nation."[8] But the citizens who do participate primarily represent interest groups, local municipalities, and government agencies. The evidence clearly points to a need to draw into the advisory committees and public hearings groups that are usually "disconnected" from politics, and to increase the available information on the Council so that more people would feel competent enough to take part. Even so, the present committee system is a useful initial foundation on which to build.

Assessment of the Development Framework

Of all the outcomes of the Metropolitan Council, the Development Framework is probably the most ambitious undertaking to date. The magnitude of this plan and its implementation process are unparalleled in the United States. The Council has not only drawn a MUSA line to channel the expansion of future metropolitan services and growth into predetermined areas, it has also established a framework within which it can make decisions about capital expenditures for metropolitan services, A-95 referrals for federal grant requests, allocation of subsidized housing throughout the metropolis, and a number of other important matters. In the Council's own perspective, the key to the Development Framework is the ability to limit growth in the rural service area while channeling growth into the urban service area and the freestanding growth centers.

Although the shelves of metropolitan planning agencies abound with comprehensive land-use plans that nobody paid any subsequent attention to, a number of factors have been coinciding in recent years to make the Metropolitan Council planners think that they have a reasonable chance to accomplish the growth-channeling goals of the Development Framework. The most important of these factors is that the Council has been given more authority and implementation tools to control land use than has been given to any other metropolitan planning agency in the country. Also supportive is the fact that the demographic environment is much more fortuitous than it has ever been. The population growth of the Twin Cities region has slowed considerably during the 1970s, adding fewer than 100,000 people between 1970 and 1977. If this slow rate of growth persists, it will be much easier to limit the growth of the rural areas. Additionally, the political conditions for controlling growth are more favorable than they have ever been. The concept itself is no longer considered subversive. The well-publicized financial crises of New York City lend support to the argument that growth control can be used to hold down public expenditures. The increasing vulnerability of the Upper Midwest region to petroleum shortages tends to make political officials more sensitive to curbing the waste of gasoline, and controlling suburban sprawl is often viewed as one way of doing this. For all these reasons, Council planners feel that the growth-channeling features of the Development Framework have bright prospects for success.

Since the major tool for accomplishing the Development Framework is the metropolitan land-planning process which extends over a three-year period until July 1, 1980, it is still too early to tell whether the plan is being achieved. But some preliminary assessments can be made on the basis of annual population estimates and household-formation data that are published each year by the Metropolitan Council demographer (see Tables 6-1 and 6-2). These tables show the population and household unit formations for the fully developed areas, the area of planned urbanization, the rural area, and the freestanding growth centers for the periods immediately preceding and following the adoption of the Development Framework in 1975. The household formations are operationalized by the number of new residential-unit building permits. When there was any doubt about whether the MUSA line brought a municipality into the urban services area, that municipality was considered as part of the metropolitan urban services area, rather than the rural services area. This has the effect of overstating growth in the area of planned urbanization and understating growth in the rural area.

There are some limitations in these data. The population estimates for 1977 are made on a different basis than the estimates for 1975, and the data for household unit formations include only a year and a half since the adoption of the Development Framework in 1975. Since the major implementation tool, the land-planning process, was barely starting during this period, the first two years

Table 6-1. Population Distribution by Planning Area

Planning Area	1970			1975			1977		
	Number	Percentage	Cumulative Percentage	Number	Percentage	Cumulative Percentage	Number	Percentage	Cumulative Percentage
Fully developed area.........	1,048,748	55.9%	55.9%	1,031,013	50.8%	50.8%	954,030	48.3%	48.3%
Area of planned urbanization...	667,524	35.6	91.5	799,282	39.3	90.1	808,950	41.0	89.3
Freestanding growth centers..	66,508	3.6	95.1	81,240	4.0	94.1	84,020	4.3	93.6
Rural area	91,832	4.9	100.0	119,801	5.9	100.0	126,470	6.4	100.0
Total	1,874,612			2,031,336			1,973,470		

Source: Metropolitan Council, *Population Estimates for 1970, 1975, 1977.*

Note: The apparent decline from 1975 to 1977 is a statistical anomaly caused by an adjustment in estimation methods after 1975. The Metropolitan Council staff believes that a small increase actually took place during this period. This does not substantially affect the percentage distribution in each of the four planning areas.

Table 6-2. Formation of New Household Units in the Minneapolis-St. Paul
Seven-County Region: 1971-74 and 1975-76

Planning Area	Predevelopment Framework, 1971-74			Postdevelopment Framework, 1975-76		
	Units	Percentage	Cumulative Percentage	Units	Percentage	Cumulative Percentage
Fully developed area	9,422	13.2%	13.2%	1,711	12.2%	12.2%
Area of planned urbanization . . .	49,165	68.7	81.9	9,266	66.2	78.4
Freestanding growth centers. . .	5,037	7.0	88.9	1,088	7.8	86.2
Rural area	7,955	11.1	100.0	1,931	13.8	100.0
Total	71,579			13,996		
Average. . . .	17,895 units annually			9,331 units annually		

Source: Metropolitan Council, *Housing Unit Estimates and Inventory* for the years 1971, 1972, 1973, 1974, 1975 and January-June 1976.

may not be a fair test of the efficacy of the Development Framework. Nevertheless, the plan was highly publicized. All municipal officials were advised that the plan existed, that the Council intended to restrict development in the designated rural areas, that the local municipalities would have to construct comprehensive plans consistent with this objective, and that the metropolitan services would not be extended into the rural areas. In other words, the growth-channeling plan was well known and the initial implementation steps had been taken. For these reasons, it is not innappropriate to ask whether the Development Framework is beginning to affect growth patterns.

The data in Tables 6-1 and 6-2 suggest that the plan to date has had little impact on growth patterns. The percentages of growth and population in the rural areas since passage of the plan, whether measured by population or by household unit formations, do not differ markedly from the percentage of growth before the Framework was adopted. If anything, the rural portion of the growth *increased* rather than decreased after passage of the plan.

Although it is still too early in the Development Framework implementation process to conclude from the data in Tables 6-1 and

6-2 that the growth-control plan is not yet working, this possibility should be taken seriously by Twin Cities policy makers. Whether or not the data in Tables 6-1 and 6-2 constitute a valid test of the Development Framework, they do point out the need to recognize some weaknesses in the existing implementation process. First, the MUSA line appears to be very flexible. As the local municipalities draft their own comprehensive plans, some adjustments in the MUSA line will have to be made. The planning process established in 1976 is still untested. Although the first phase of it has run smoothly, the test will come when one or more municipalities' comprehensive plans attempt to make a major extension of the line. There will also be major attempts to increase some communities' share of the sewer-system capacity. And there will surely be attempts to tie particular rural subdivisions into the MWCC interceptors in places that are currently prohibited by Metropolitan Council policies.

A second weakness lies in the attempted to use upgraded septic-tank regulations to limit the population densities of the rural area. As indicated earlier, the MPCA's anticipated septic-tank regulations will not be mandatory, and this will seriously weaken the Council's ability to limit population density in the rural region. The Council at this writing is planning to incorporate a density criterion in its review procedures for development in the rural service area. But even if this is put into practice, and even if metropolitan septic-tank regulations are upgraded, there are no provisions for the possibility that someone may find an economically feasible way to market sanitary disposal systems that require neither septic tanks nor sewers. Such a system would make density regulations totally obsolete.

Closely related to the second weakness is a third. As noted earlier, the Green Acres Law was passed by the Legislature to preserve agricultural land. But several deficiencies have been found in its ability to do this, and some Council planners suspect that the law has been more beneficial to the land developers than it has to farmers attempting to keep their land in production.

A fourth problem with protecting the rural area from development concerns the nature of what the Council is trying to protect. Although the southern and western portions of the metropolitan area contain some of the most fertile agricultural land in the nation, the northern portions tend to have very sandy soil that is not prime agricultural land. Politically, the Council is in a very awkward position when it tells the people in those areas that they must not develop their land even though the land has very limited value for farming. It may not be in those persons' best financial interests to leave their land undeveloped, and they may be able to exert considerable political and moral pressure on the Council to modify its Development Framework.

A fifth problem with the Development Framework is that is has no means to control leapfrog development beyond the bounds of the seven-county area. Evidence that this is occurring exists on several fronts. The Twin Cities SMSA has been expanded geographically to include three more counties as a result of growth in them. Although the population of the seven-county area grew little from 1970 to 1977, dramatic percentage increases have occurred in the populations of the counties immediately adjacent to the seven counties. In some of these localities there has been a rapid influx of trailer courts and single-family homes relying on septic tanks in soils that are not suitable for them. As the demand for public services increases in these areas, they are facing the same kinds of problems faced in the seven-county region before the Metropolitan Council was created.

Finally, a sixth problem may exist in that most of the Council's implementation tools are negative rather than positive. The Council seems to be in the position of trying to prevent other actors from doing things that the Council considers undesirable. Little progress has been made in developing positive tools that would make other actors react to Council initiatives. The concepts of land banking and municipal development corporations do not seem to have gathered much support even though they are part of the Development Framework chapter. Most of the goals of the Fully Developed Area Task Force report seem to be couched in terms of ideals rather than practical programs.[9] If the Council is to redevelop the central cities and curb growth in the rural areas, it probably needs to devote more attention to positive actions to balance off its already impressive collection of negative powers.

Anticipating the Future of the Twin Cities

Although all governments must be able to solve problems and settle conflicts, they should also be able to anticipate the future and plan for it. This latter task is of particular concern to the Metropolitan Council, which is a nonoperating policy-making agency, intended to be free from daily managerial details. It was compelled in its early days to produce solutions to immediate problems such as sewage disposal, but in recent years the Council has been moving toward its long-range planning functions.

To anticipate the future, one must be able to project current trends for a decade or more, forecast social and technological innovations, and integrate these developments with one another to identify their mutual effects. Anticipating the future also implies watching for new opportunities to improve the quality of life. A modern metropolis is an intricate web of both problems and opportunities that are not the clear responsibility of any one government or private organization. Indeed, they frequently are not even recognized until the best moment for beginning action on them has passed. The Metropolitan Council's long-run contributions to the governance of the Twin Cities region depend heavily on whether it can successfully anticipate problems and opportunities so that action can be taken on them at the optimum time.

What are the most significant trends and developments that should be anticipated? The following discussion identifies only a few that have been most clearly analyzed in the past several years. Trend data and qualitative judgments are abundant, owing to the research of the Commission on Minnesota's Future, the Upper Midwest Council, the Minnesota State Demographer, and the staff of the Metropolitan Council.[10] Although they have used somewhat different methods and begun with different questions, their findings are generally consistent with each other.

First, the demographic projections point to a slow population growth in the region. The Metropolitan Council forecasts a seven-county total of 2,036,000 in 1980, and 2,489,000 in 2000—a 26 percent rise from the estimated population of 1,973,000 in 1977.[11] There will be an increased proportion of middle-age and elderly persons, and fewer children. There will be more household units— families, couples, or single persons living alone—but the average household will be smaller, declining from 3.2 persons per household in 1970 to 2.6.[12] The population losses of Minneapolis and St. Paul are expected to taper off as more households locate there. The older suburbs will stabilize or decline, and major growth is envisioned for the less urbanized suburbs inside the MUSA line.

A second set of important trends concerns natural resources, particularly energy and water. Rising costs and sporadic but growing shortages of oil and natural gas, together with constraints on coal mining and electrical generation, have already required economic adjustments and led to social hardships. This trend will continue, spawning more numerous and serious political conflicts for the metropolitan area as well as for the nation as a whole. Most decisions about costs and supplies are made by state and national governments and private corporations. However, regional institutions do have the opportunity of making decisions on the internal distribution and conservation of energy as well as developing local energy sources through new techniques such as resource recovery. Railroad lines from the coal fields of the Dakotas run through the Twin Cities, and this means that any national programs to boost coal production would have direct consequences for the Twin Cities economy. For these reasons, the Metropolitan Council may need to concern itself with the regional implications for the energy policies of the Minnesota Energy Agency and of the U.S. Department of Energy.

In spite of the presence of many lakes, three major rivers, and a large underground aquifer, water supply and quality will be a growing problem as water demands grow. Ground and surface water used by cities and industry will need to be monitored increasingly. Ultimately, some kind of apportionment plan may become necessary to settle competing claims on the same water sources, and responsibility for drafting this plan may fall on the Metropolitan Council. That, in turn, will affect its existing policies for waste management, land use, and environmental preservation.

Third, new forms of land-use conflict are likely to emerge. As changes occur in the social and economic characteristics of certain neighborhoods of the fully developed areas, there will be demands and opportunities to provide more or better space for industry, business, residences, and recreation. At the same time, there will be pressures to conserve natural open spaces and historically significant districts in the face of competing uses for them. Added to that, energy constraints will make it more imperative to use existing urban land and buildings more efficiently. The governance of land in the metropolitan area, as in the nation as a whole, is more oriented to preventing or restricting specific uses than it is to making positive developmental changes. This latter effort may need to become a major part of the *Development Guide* in the future, at least for some parts of the region.

Fourth, new technological developments have always spurred governmental reactions, but some anticipation of these is becoming more important. For example, many observers predict the demise of the private automobile and its replacement by new forms of mass transit. Yet, it is more likely that the use of cars—albeit smaller, more efficient cars powered by fuels other than gasoline—will increase as residential and commercial land uses become less dense.[13] A counterpossibility is that sophisticated and universal communications links will replace much of the current business and educational travel. The technology now exists to convey both voices and data to and from every home and workplace in the region.[14] To exploit and manage this potential requires an equally sophisticated management system that, whether publicly or privately owned, is fully accountable to the public. Should either or both trends intensify, extensive public planning and action will be required on a regional scale to supplement any state and national policies that are adopted.

Growing out of the above social, resource, and technological changes will be new and altered demands for policy responses. For example, educational resources are now heavily devoted to children, youth, and persons about to begin careers. But as the proportion of persons in these age groups declines, the allocation of educational resources may be shifted to the large number of persons in mid- and post-career situations seeking further education. As these reallocations occur, there will be an increase in the need to coordinate the plans of school districts, higher education authorities, private schools and colleges, and other educational institutions.

To cite another issue, there is likely to be an intense search for new housing forms. The popular single-family detached home on its quarter-acre lot is too expensive and prodigal in its use of land and energy to be the major solution to future housing needs. Yet, most contemporary apartments and town houses lack appeal to a society that values its privacy and expects more room and amenities than satisfied its parents. In addition to present efforts to expand housing opportunities for low-income persons and minorities, there will have to be a blend of incentives and restraints to shape housing development to these conditions while producing enough to supply the growing number of households.

A policy area that transcends many specific issues is that of securing a just measure of equality of services and opportunities to all persons. Various "distinct" groups that have been denied these by public decision (or neglect) or social pressures are now rising to claim their equality and occasionally a compensating advantage. For blacks, women, Spanish-speaking persons, and homosexuals, the issue is well publicized although still far from resolved. But these trends also will involve the claims of children, persons who are mentally or physically handicapped, and those with inadequate education. For all these, a longer list of "rights" will be presented. Often, action to secure such rights can best be organized on a regional scale (if not higher) and will challenge the implementation of the Metropolitan Council's Social Framework policies.

Future developments in many other policy areas could be mentioned, but these few suggest the complexity of the task. None is independent of the others. Reduced water quality increases medical costs. More expensive energy restrains travel behavior. Better mid-career education may improve economic opportunities for minorities and the poorly educated and in turn improve their ability to afford quality housing. No public or private plan could possibly account for all these interrelationships, but there needs to be a regional "early warning system" to identify problems and opportunities that rise above some threshhold of significance. The political scientist Grover Starling has called for the creation of "look-out institutions"—agencies autonomous of other units of government that could indicate various possible futures and suggest to decision makers what specific actions should be taken to bring them about.[15] The Metropolitan Council has begun to undertake the first function and has the potential to take on the second.

An additional role for the Metropolitan Council is to assess the impact of state and national government policies on the region. In spite of rhetoric about "creative federalism," the American federal system is becoming more centralized in many ways. In the field of energy policy, for example, a serious danger exists that local programs to conserve fuel or develop new energy sources may be negated by national policies. Minnesota is especially vulnerable to the location of pipelines tapping into the Alaskan petroleum and natural gas reserves. In such situations, the Council can help mobilize political power to speak for the region's energy interests and work for alternate policies.

A final consideration is the future relationship of government to the private sector. Businesses and nonprofit organizations are significant providers of "public" goods and services, from natural gas and nursing care to taxi service and technical education. Metropolitan Council policies envision a continued dependence on them. The Commission on Minnesota's Future, in its final report, asserted that

government must become more of a facilitator than a provider. That is, government should be responsible for evaluating the needs of the state and seeing that they are met, though not necessarily providing them. It is becoming physically impossible for government to provide all the services that meet the full range of human needs. The focus of government attention must be on monitoring and evaluating the forces of change, anticipating needs, and guiding the decision-making system.[16]

These activities of government can include contracting with private agencies to supply some kinds of services, granting financial aid to begin a new private program, research into new possibilities to generate information that can be applied by others, sharing buildings and facilities, and setting standards to ensure adequate private performance in essential functions. Ideally, the private sector will often take the initiative, especially when likely profits are at stake. But these efforts may have to be channeled or restrained when essential public or private interests could be harmed. All these cooperative measures can be applied in solar energy development, for example, or in the rehabilitation of criminal offenders.

In any such public-private ventures, great care must be taken to ensure that the ventures primarily accomplish the public good rather than enrich the private entrepreneurs who contract with the government. It would not take a great deal of historical research to compile a substantial list of public-private ventures pervaded by scandalous lack of governmental accountability over the program—Section 235 housing programs, certain Medicare practices, and the establishment of fictitious laboratory reports under Medicaid and other federal health-care programs. In all these areas the many honest entrepreneurs find their reputations endangered by the activities of the few dishonest ones. Even when public-private ventures have been administered honestly, the results have often been disappointing. The federally assisted Cedar-Riverside and Jonathan "New Town" projects have failed to live up to their bright promise. State and federally assisted projects in Minneapolis and St. Paul have redeveloped the two downtowns,[17] but have done little to stem the population outflow from these cities, and the Metropolitan Council indicates that about half the residential housing still needs rehabilitation.[18] In light of this history, a serious study is needed of the conditions under which public-private ventures are successful. As a planning and policy-making body, the Metropolitan Council would be an ideal institution for conducting such a study and establishing some practical guidelines.

Current Issues

Although the Metropolitan Council has gained considerable legitimacy and has taken very effective steps toward solving the more severe area-wide problems such as sewage, serious metropolitan issues remain unresolved as of this writing. Some are very specific, such as implementing the 1976 Land-Planning Act, developing water-resource management policies, and drafting the Social Framework policies. These presumably will be on the Council's work program over the next few years. In addition, there are broader questions. Some, such as whether the Council should be elected, surface every legislative session. Others, such as the permeability and bias of the Council's policy-making process, have not yet been placed on any official decision-making agendas and thus may not be obvious issues. But they are at least latent issues in the sense that they expose some basic contradictions and inconsistencies between what the Council is supposedly trying to accomplish and what in fact is occurring. Six such issues will be introduced briefly here—appropriateness of the Council's power, accountability, permeability of the policy-making process, meaning of the metropolitan policies, the

Council as a guider of or reactor to metropolitan developments, and the Council's ability to monitor the impacts of its policies.

Are the Council's Powers Sufficient?

The 1976 League of Women Voters survey cited earlier indicates some division of opinion on whether the Council's powers ought to be expanded, reduced, or kept the same. There are two aspects to this question—whether the Council should receive powers in areas for which it has no current responsibilities and whether its authority should be strengthened on matters for which it has already been given some responsibilities.

Two examples of significant functional areas in which the Council currently lacks policy-making authority are education and the new sports stadium. Public education probably accounts for more governmental expenditures than any other single function in the metropolitan area. Education is also tied intimately to many of the other policy areas that concern the Council. The most obvious of these is the efficient management of school facilities. Each time a school building is constructed it affects development plans, sewer-system capacities, housing patterns, and several other key policy areas of the *Metropolitan Development Guide*. Of special concern is the construction of new school buildings in districts that are growing, while only a few miles away buildings are being closed in neighboring districts whose enrollments are declining. The school districts must submit construction plans to the Council for review, but the Council has no authority to hold up construction. The Legislature recognizes the need for planning and coordination between school districts. But rather than subordinate development plans to the Metropolitan Council and the other regional development commissions outstate, the Legislature created Educational Cooperative Service Units (ECSU), which were given general data-gathering, planning, and coordinating functions. In other words, education represents one functional area into which the Council's authority has not been extended. This is true even in those aspects that directly affect its own development policies, to say nothing of a role in meeting the future educational needs identified earlier in this chapter.

A different problem was presented to the Council when the Legislature created the Metropolitan Sports Facilities Commission (MSFC) in 1977. The issue of building a new professional sports stadium had roiled every legislative session since 1973, and the site was only one of several controversial questions the lawmakers could not answer. The MSFC was charged with deciding, first, whether a new stadium should be built or the existing Metropolitan Stadium in Bloomington remodeled. If it chose to build a new facility, it would have to choose the site, subject to certain conditions set in the legislation. Finally the MSFC would own and operate that and other sports facilities on a continuing basis. The Metropolitan Council had not been directly involved in this issue before, although a 1973 report of one of its task forces had recommended such a resolution.

The MSFC is not governed like the other metropolitan commissions (MTC, MWCC, and MPOSC). Its members are appointed by the governor, not the Metropolitan Council. Although the Council has power to review and veto its capital and operating budgets, it cannot reject a site or design selection unless it violates the legislative conditions. The Council is charged with reporting to the MSFC only if the final two potential sites are not consistent with the *Development Guide* and other metropolitan policies. The Commission thereby has been given an autonomy that is contrary to the pattern established by the 1974 Metropolitan Reorganization Act. The only precedent for such autonomy of a metropolitan public function was the Legislature's decision in 1969 to establish a state zoo in the region. It has been under a State Zoological Board throughout the period, although the Metropolitan Council set criteria for its location and development program. The Legislature may, however, bring the MSFC under the Council's policy control in the future, after the politically volatile issue of choosing a stadium site has been decided.

In addition to the question of the Council's possible authority over educational and sports facilities, a more immediate issue is whether the Council's authority is sufficient in areas for which it already has responsibility. For example, in discussing the Development Framework and the land-planning process, several weaknesses were noted in the Council's implementation powers. Whether these powers are sufficient is a question that the Legislature will have to continue asking.

Whatever the feeling about extending the Council's powers, it seems unlikely that much extension will take place over the next few years. Between 1974 and 1977 the Council received broad extensions of authority, and it seems likely that the next several years will be ones of consolidating these powers, attempting to implement them, and evaluating their effectiveness. Until this process is well advanced, it seems unlikely that the Council will request any new major increments to its authority or that the Legislature will grant any, barring some regional emergency.

Is the Council Accountable?

At the heart of the question over the Council's power is the question of accountability. Is the Metropolitan Council going to be a government of governments or a government of people? Advocates of election feel that elected Council members would become accountable to the voters and transform the Council into a government of people. This is, they claim, most consistent with the democratic principle of representative government. Advocates of what is perhaps the most enervating appointive method would have the Council members appointed directly by the local governments in their districts. This would presumably make the Council members much more attentive to the desires of these local officials and make the Council clearly a government of governments.

When the Council was created in 1967 the question of accountability was a dominant one, and the Legislature by a very narrow margin chose to have the members appointed by the governor. The issue has resurfaced in every subsequent legislative session, and each time the election proposal drew much but not quite majority support. Even if there were clear majority support among legislators for this principle, there are divisive questions concerning how the election should be conducted. Should the election be publicly financed? Should the chairman be elected at large, appointed by the governor, or selected by the Council members from among themselves? Should the terms of office be overlapping? And how long should the terms be? in 1977 different bills in each house came up with various combinations of answers to these questions, but no specific plan won majority support, and the Legislature put off the question for another year.

Supporters of the present appointment method rely on several arguments. The first view is that appointment by the governor (with Senate confirmation) is the best way to keep the Council accountable to the public, because the governor and the Legislature can exercise continued vigilance over the Council's exercise of its powers. The second argument in favor of the present appointment method is based on the fear that making the Council elective would increase its political autonomy and its power. A third argument is that the present system has functioned well and has fairly consistently produced Council members who take an area-wide view of metropolitan problems. If the Council members were to be chosen by district voters or by local officials, they would tend to view their responsibilities much more parochially and become advocates of exclusively local interests. The League of Women Voters appears to have been swayed by this argument, and in 1977 for the first time it publicly urged the retention of the Council as an appointive body.

Because of the one person-one vote principle in the apportionment of Council districts, most members live in the central cities and the inner suburbs. Officials of the less populated but fast-growing "outer ring" suburbs claim that this denies them adequate representation, especially since they experience most of the impact of the Council's growth-control decisions. Further, some of their Council members have had central-city-oriented business or professional interests despite their residence in the outer suburbs. Many local officials also feel that appointment by the governor ensures a Council membership that shares a metropolitan-wide philosophy rather than a loyalty to local government. These feelings are no doubt exacerbated by the fact that both governors since 1971 have been Democrats, and the outlying suburbs usually vote Republican. The officials in these areas are skeptical that the Democratic governors can appoint Council members who will truly represent their interests. Some of them support a plan introduced in 1976 that would reduce the representation of the fully developed areas in the Council, increase the representation of the outlying suburbs, and have the Council members appointed by the local officials.

Most of these varied positions on selecting Council members can be traced to one of the two preferences indicated earlier—the Council as a government of governments or the Council as a government of people. Both viewpoints indicate considerable confusion about whom the Council is presently accountable to. In great measure the Council is directly accountable to the Legislature which has granted much of its authority. The Council is also partially accountable to federal agencies that control funds and impose legal sanctions in fields such as water pollution, health planning, transportation, housing, and others. It is also partially accountable to local officials whose noncooperation can torpedo Council intentions. Additionally, most Council members exhibit a sense of responsbility to the metropolitan-minded community elites who write editorials, join Citizens League task forces, lobby before the Legislature, introduce resolutions at political party, labor union, and civic group conventions, and in general exercise considerable influence in defining the agendas for public agencies. It is interesting to note, as one surveys the various interest groups that serve as clients of the Council, that in light of all the debate over selection methods there is no evidence to suggest any realistic accountability of Council members to the person who presently appoints them—the governor. In the entire history of the Council, the governors have intervened very little in its deliberations.

It is difficult to predict how elections would affect the accountability of the Council. Unless publicly financed, elections would probably increase the Council's attentiveness to real-estate developers and construction trade unions that would have considerable incentive to make large campaign contributions. Election would not negate the current institutional and legal ties between the Council and the Legislature, the federal government, and the local governments. Nor would an elected Council be likely to eclipse the Legislature. Probably the only way to find out whether the election process would accomplish all the things hoped for by its supporters and feared by its opponents would be to make the Council elective. What makes the Legislature hesitant to do this is that unlike the other increments of power, which could be monitored, evaluated, and adjusted over the years, election is an irreversible step. Once elections were established it would be politically impossible to revoke the public's choice of Council members, even if a serious failure or scandal occurred. Even altering the terms of election could be extremely difficult.[19]

How Permeable Is the Policy-Making Process?

Related to accountability is the permeability and bias of the Council's policy-making processes. The Council leans heavily on its staff and advisory committees. The advisory committee process, as discussed earlier, goes to great lengths to ensure that all interested parties have some chance to influence the policy that eventually results. Proposed policies are brought to the attention of the public, local governments, interest groups, and other interested parties long before they reach the draft stage for public hearing. Policies go through several revised drafts which enable interested parties to object to policies they dislike or to insert policies they desire. One consequence of this has been to give the *Development Guide* chapters a grab-bag appearance of including enough items to give symbolic assurance to all interests and to reach a low enough common denominator that the policies will get broad political support.

The observer must question, however, whether this process is really as open as it seems. Currently, metropolitan policies appear to be most responsive to input from interest groups, Council staff members, local government officials, and functional specialists at other levels of government. The citizen generalist has little influence. Although the advisory committee system may be more open than those in other metropolitan areas, it still tends to be dominated by government officials and interest-group members. The appointive process to these committees needs more study, but it is doubtful that isolated, unsponsored individuals could dominate any advisory committee. Whether by design or by accident, the advisory committee system seems to co-opt vocal local-government officials. As these officials get on advisory committees and begin working on metropolitan problems, they tend to become more supportive of the Council and help to smooth relations between it and the local governments. Outside the advisory committee process there appears to be little mechanism for the individual citizen to have input on Council policies. All proposed policies are subjected to public hearings before they are adopted. However, if one compares the drafts of the *Development Guide* chapters prepared for public hearings with the final chapters adopted after the hearings, one finds very few changes. The isolated citizens who object to particular policies at public hearings are unlikely to have much influence. From this, it appears that the Council's policy-making process is shielded from unorganized citizen demands. It is doubtful that direct election of members would change this very much. Election would most likely add to the Council's legitimacy without making it much more accountable to the citizens.

The categories of people who lack or think they lack representation in the Council's policy-making process are not small—Native Americans, Chicanos, lower-class whites who are left out of he labor-union complex, and officials of very small suburban governments. One should probably add the black community, although the Metropolitan Council has usually included at least one black member. It would be important to study the process of selecting the advisory committee members to learn to what extent these categories of people lack access. Their representation appears to be left largely to upper-middle-class professionals who are eager to deal with the problems of the poor.

In defense of the Metropolitan Council's attempts to be accessible to the public, it must be pointed out that the kind of issues that regularly come before the Council rarely elicit broad popular interest. Public reaction to an A-95 review discussion or a debate over a *Development Guide* chapter pales in comparison to public reaction to immediate crises such as closing a school or regulating pornography that come before school boards and city councils. The Council does make a serious effort to communicate with the public at large. Its weekly newsletter is mailed to 3,000 recipients and its monthly letter to over 10,000 others.[20] Thousands of other people are on specialized mailing lists for policy areas such as housing or criminal justice. The number of people volunteering to serve on advisory committees has also reached into the thousands. A critical problem facing all contemporary, large-scale democratic governments is precisely that of gaining an optimal level of mass participation in regular policy making. Because of the peculiar nature of the Metropolitan Council and the kinds of issues it handles, citizen participation presents a particularly difficult challenge.

What Do Council Policies Mean?

A further problem with Council policies concerns their clarity and intent. As of mid-1977, most of the policies in the protection open space chapter appear to be in limbo while the staff begins work on a water-resource management chapter. Also, as indicated earlier, some policies are so broad that they seem to be little more than symbolic statements, while others are very detailed. Consistency is also a problem. Although the Council has paid increasing attention to eliminating inconsistencies between chapters, some are still apparent. For example, housing policies put a strong emphasis on restraining the rising costs of new construction and on expanding housing opportunities for lower-income groups in suburban areas. However, the Development Framework limits the suburban space that is open to extensive home construction. And rather than prorating the costs of new sewer extensions over the entire metropolitan area, the Council established a Service Availability Charge of several hundred dollars which must be paid when each new house receives a building permit. The latter two policies are likely to inflate housing costs, frustrating the goal of holding down these costs.

When a citizen of the metropolitan area looks at Council policies, he or she may easily become confused. One is tempted to paraphrase George Orwell and say that all the policies mean something, but some mean more than others. The problem for the citizen is figuring out which policies mean the most and what their effects will be on him or her. The Council has not effectively communicated what it is trying to accomplish with many of them. The Development Framework is probably the most coherent statement tying together its goals in the area of physical development. The Council has the same hopes for its Social Framework, but the much larger number of policies and implementing agencies makes that task harder yet.

Is the Council a Leader or Follower?

In the earlier discussions of the Development Framework and the disputes over transit planning, some questions were raised about the Council's ability to impose its policies in a positive way rather than simply exercising a negative review over other agencies and governments. It is still an open question whether the Development Framework, ambitious as it is, can really guide future growth or will simply accommodate existing growth forces. Since the MUSA line is drawn beyond the present boundaries of urban sprawl, it does not really inhibit growth in the currently urbanizing areas within the seven-county region. As pointed out earlier, if development is to be restricted from the communities just beyond the MUSA line, then the major beneficiaries will be the cities inside that line. They will be likely to get the growth that would spill beyond those boundaries if no controls existed. If this is the case, then one must ask whether the MUSA line is really altering future trends. Or is it simply reinforcing current trends and freezing them for the next fifteen years?

It is, of course, too early to answer that question, but it is of vital importance to the metropolitan policy makers. Over the past ten years the Council's role has slowly solidified into that of providing an arena within which area-wide problems can be solved. It presents the Legislature with workable policies that have a consensus or at least majority political support of the dominant interests involved. Achieving consensus, co-opting local government officials, building support for policies, and responding to interest-group pressures are, of course, critical leadership functions. But they are not the same as guiding developments.

These characteristics of the Council's policy-making process lead one to question its dynamism as the guider of metropolitan innovation in areas not covered by the Development Framework. As one group of observers noted, the Council's "process of policy administration has always been reactive. The policies are set forth and then the Council responds to others as they bring in their proposals."[21] This reactive style results, perhaps, from its tendency to take a problem-solving and crisis-management approach to metropolitan governance.[22] The first solid waste chapter of the *Development Guide*, for example, ignored the possibility of resource recovery, and that position was not revised until after the Legislature passed an act in 1976 giving the Council authority in that field. Despite staff prodding to develop water-resource policies, the Council put off doing so until the drought of 1976-77 stimulated sufficient political support. In 1976 the Association of Metropolitan Municipalities responded to complaints from some local officials tha the Metropolitan Council was exceeding its authority and made an intensive comparison of its actions and its legal mandates. The Association found, however, that the Council had been very careful not to exceed its legal authority.[23]

In sum, the Council seems to operate much more effectively as an arena for resolving policy differences and achieving consensus than it does as a policy innovator. This approach has the advantage of identifying and possibly alleviating the symptoms that one perceives as problems. At the same time, this problem-solving approach offers no assurance that major problems can be anticipated and dealt with before they have to be "solved" at much higher costs. Nor is it a method of penetrating beyond the perceived problems to the underlying causes and conditions. Interest groups tend to play important roles in defining these problems and are well represented on the Council's advisory committees. This may mean that side effects unimportant to these groups will be ignored, and that future opportunities not anticipated by any organized group attract no attention.[24]

Can the Council Monitor the Impacts of Its Policies?

A common charge made against modern government is that it does not, or cannot, learn the results and impacts of its policies in time to correct its mistakes and shortcomings. The U.S. federal government, in particular, has launched vast and ambitious programs with reasonably clear objectives but has devoted little effort to evaluating these programs as they were implemented. Thus, it lacked means to determine whether the objectives were being met or where faults existed. In the case of its efforts in housing, medicare, and family assistance, the problems had to be publicized by private groups and the press.

Because the Metropolitan Council makes policy but does not directly implement it, the Council has both advantages and disadvantages compared with an administering agency. It is not burdened with the details of bus route patronage or the diameter of sewer pipe, and so can give its energies to the data-collecting and monitoring tasks. Too, it does not have vested interests in concealing shortcomings or inflating successes. Above all, it can grasp the interrelationships between programs carried out by different agencies that might be ignored or suppressed by interagency politics.

Despite these strengths, the Council may easily concern itself too much in planning and policy making to involve itself sufficiently in assessment of policy outcomes. To "look back" in this way might violate the ethos of an inherently forward-looking agency. Negative evaluations might also threaten the Metropolitan Council's relations with the operating agencies, particularly those not under its policy controls. Finally, it may have more difficulty obtaining timely and accurate data that could be generated by those who are closely involved in administration.

Over the years the Council has compiled an enormous stock of data. Its 1977 *State of the Region* report was only a capsule summary of these. The current state of affairs in many policy areas can be described and measured with quantitative indicators of all kinds, to aid in pointing out conditions that may need public attention. The most recent policy chapter on health is a good example of this. What is inherently much harder to do is to determine the impact of a specific health program on a specific set of clients in a certain period of time. When the relation between the "cause" and the hoped-for "effect" is obscure, policy planners as well as evaluators are left in the dark. To be sure, the effects of an increase in bus service to a particular community or of emergency telephone service can be fairly obvious, but the educational impact of cable television or of a neighborhood-based rehabilitation program for youthful offenders cannot be charted in the short run. As the effects of the Council's policies multiply, it needs to increase its capacity to monitor and evaluate them at the same rate.

Transferability

Despite the critical questions raised above about the Council and the Minnesota system of metropolitan governance, the authors believe that on balance this Twin Cities experiment has enjoyed considerable success. When governmental experiments prove successful, there is often a spate of attempts to transfer the experiments into other locales. And the question naturally arises whether the Twin Cities approach to metropolitan governance is transferable elsewhere. Governments have a tendency to borrow from one another.[25] When planning-program-budgeting systems (PPBS) were in vogue during the 1960s, for example, governments at all levels hastened to implement their own versions of program budgeting. When "Sunset laws" became popular during the middle 1970s, again rarely did a year pass without a number of states enacting time limits on some programs or agencies. Will a similar thing happen with the Twin Cities approach to metropolitan governance?

Before examining this question of transferability, two caveats must be given. First, although the Metropolitan Council has worked well and been accepted in the Twin Cities, some other areas may not need to adopt it. Miami-Dade County, for example, has brought under a single county government a population and land area comparable to that of Minneapolis-St. Paul. City-county consolidated governments in Jacksonville, Nashville, and Indianapolis are busy trying to make their own governmental experiments work and would have no particular reason to change directions at this point. Similarly, Houston, Phoenix, and many other cities of the Southwest that operate under liberal annexation laws are able to bring most developing land under direct city control. In other metropolitan areas, federal initiatives such as the A-95 power, the creation of metropolitan-wide health-service agencies, and water-quality-management agencies under the Section 208 programs have led to the formation of councils of government (COGs), which perform many of the same functions now being performed in the Twin Cities by the Metropolitan Council. Some of these COGs do not operate very well and barely hold together. In 1975, for example, three counties withdrew from the Puget Sound Council of Governments and only rejoined after the federal government threatened to withhold certain federal funds subject to A-95 reviews.[26] It is dubious that such a region would want the centralized policy-making system that exists in the Twin Cities. There are no comparative studies to determine whether highly centralized metropolitan agencies for coordinating federal programs do a better job than the highly decentralized COGs. So, although the Metropolitan Council gets numerous inquiries about itself and is the subject of much interest, it is still an open question whether any other region even wants to make a wholesale tranfer of the Twin Cities structure to their regions.

A second caveat concerns what is transferable. The *processes* of developing a strong metropolitan policy-making capability are probably more transferable than are the particular structures of the Metropolitan Council.[27] As noted in Chapter 2, the key feature of the creation and evolution of the Metropolitan Council was *incrementalism*. Three aspects of this incremental approach are directly relevant to questions of transferability. First, the accomplishment of metropolitan reform requires the existence of influential citizens who adopt a metropolitan perspective on certain problems. In the Twin Cities, a number of legislators since the early 1960s have had such a perspective on metropolitan service issues. Probably more critical, however, was the Citizens League, which has served as an effective forum for researching and publicizing metropolitan issues and policy alternatives.[28] Because Citizens League reports touched so many issues of metropolitan governance, they were a significant force in building support for the creation and evolution of the Metropolitan Council. More than that, it has been a useful supplement to the Council's advisory committees in institutionalizing long-term interest in metropolitan-wide problems.

At the same time that there has been a long-term continuity of civic leadership in resolving metropolitan problems, there has been a certain amount of continuity among the leadership of the Legislature. Some of the legislators who played key roles in creating the Council in 1967 also helped pass the legislation which set the stage for its continued evolution after 1967.

It may be that this continuity of both civic and legislative leadership has facilitated a consensus on the general vision of a metropolitan governance model. This model separates metropolitan policy making from the administration of governmental services. The policy-making role has been consistently reserved for the Metropolitan Council, and the delivery of services is left for the existing counties, municipalities, special districts, and metropolitan agencies. This particular model may not be appropriate for all metropolitan areas. But it does seem essential if metropolitan reform is to succeed, that enough continuity exist among the actual or potential regional politicians to build some consensus on the general direction of their reform efforts.

If the existence of some general consensus among legislative decision makers and private influentials is the first key element to the incremental approach, the second key element is the existence of a corrective feedback process. In Minnesota, each extension of the Metropolitan Council's powers was subsequently reviewed by the Legislature. Thus, for example, the Legislature in 1967 directed the Council to propose a solution to the sewer problem. When the Council's proposed solution worked, it increased the Legislature's confidence in the Council. And when the Council later fell into a stalemate with the MTC over rapid transit, the Legislature responded with the Metropolitan Reorganization Act of 1974 which reaffirmed the Council's role as the dominant policy maker. The passage of this act in turn required the appropriate legislative committees once again to monitor its implementation, to listen to interested parties, and to work out new compromises. Ultimately, this led to the Land Planning Act of 1976.

This feedback process seems to be peculiar to the legislative-dominated, incremental approaches to metropolitan reform. In regions where metropolitan reform occurred through drastic charter changes approved by the voters in referendums, there appears to have been little subsequent evolutionary change in the reformed governmental structure. This seems to be particularly true in Nashville, Jacksonville, and Baton Rouge, where city-county consolidations were established. In Miami-Dade County, the only substantial charter revision occurred in 1964; voters rejected major charter amendments in 1969 and 1972.

A third element of the Twin Cities reform process that may be transferable is the legislative role. A handful of legislators can understand the need for continuous, incremental change much more readily than several hundred thousand voters can. If voters are asked to modify the basic governmental charter every two years, it will be very difficult to avoid conveying the impression to them that the charter is basically ineffective and that the political leaders who keep coming back asking for more changes are incompetent. For this reason, legislative committees are a much more conducive forum for the incremental process than are voter referendums. The incremental process enables legislators to give limited grants of authority, to observe that limited authority being tested over a reasonable time period, and then to evaluate how the authority was exercised. In Minnesota this process helps keep the Metropolitan Council and the metropolitan agencies accountable to the Legislature. It also permits compromises that are impossible to achieve in a referendum. Voters are only allowed to vote yes or no, and they cannot weigh alternative proposals or create new combinations of possibilities that will enable enough interest groups to reach a consensus. In the absence of such a consensus-building mechanism, it is not surprising that the disappointed leaders and interest groups are able so often to convince a majority of the voters to reject the referendums.

In conclusion, if any part of the Twin Cities experiment is transferable, it is much more likely to be the process of reform rather than the total package of innovative structures. Crucial to this process are a willingness to use incremental change, the development of influential institutions, analogous to the Citizens League, that provide a forum for metropolitan-minded citizens to exercise influence, a certain amount of continuity in the civic and legislative leadership, some consensus on a general vision of what needs to be accomplished, and the willingness of legislative leaders to establish a corrective feedback relationship with metropolitan agencies.

Notes

Notes

Chapter 1

1. The Metropolitan Council, *State of the Region: The Twin Cities Metropolitan Area* (St. Paul, February 1977).

2. *Ibid.*, p. 112. This report shows only 272 governments; since its publication, a Metropolitan Sports Facilities Commission has been created.

3. See United States Bureau of the Census, *Statistical Abstract of the United States* (Washington, D.C.: U.S. Government Printing Office, 1972), pp. 851, 871, and 891.

4. For the purposes of this study, *Megalopolis* is defined as a number of metropolitan areas joined. Along the northeast seacoast forty-one SMSAs from New Hampshire to Virginia contain about 40 million people. In the Midwest, branching out from major Great Lakes cities, are thirty SMSAs with 25 million people. Population data on SMSAs are found in the United States Bureau of the Census, *County and City Data Book: 1972* (Washington, D.C.: U.S. Government Printing Office, 1972), pp. 29-587.

5. For background on the city-county consolidation in Jacksonville, see John M. De Grove, "The City of Jacksonville: Consolidation in Action," in Advisory Commission on Intergovernmental Relations, Report A-41: Volume II, *Regional Governance: Promise and Performance — Case Studies* (Washington, D.C.: U.S. Government Printing Office, 1974), pp. 19-20. For background on Miami's metropolitan reform see: Edward Sofen, *The Miami Metropolitan Experiment* (Bloomington: Indiana University Press, 1963); Aileen Lotz, "Metropolitan Dade County," in ACIR, Report A-41. On Nashville, see: Daniel R. Grant, "Urban and Suburban Nashville: A Case Study in Metropolitanism," *The Journal of Politics* 17 (February 1965); Brett W. Hawkins, *Nashville Metro: The Politics of City-County Consolidation* (Nashville, Tenn.: Vanderbilt University Press, 1966); David A. Booth, *Metropolitics: The Nashville Consolidation* (East Lansing: Institute for Community Development and Services, Michigan State University, 1963); Daniel R. Grant, "Metropolitics and Professional Political Leadership: The Case of Nashville," *Annals of the American Academy of Political and Social Science*, 353 (May 1964); Robert E. McArthur, "The Metropolitan Government of Nashville and Davidson County," in ACIR, Report A-41.

6. An older but still useful study of this problem is found in Advisory Commission on Intergovernmental Relations, *Metropolitan Social and Economic Disparities* (Washington, D.C.: U.S. Government Printing Office, 1965). For a more recent analysis, see Advisory Commission on Intergovernmental Relations, *Improving Urban America* (Washington, D.C.: U.S. Government Printing Office, 1976), Chapter 2.

7. See the decision of the California Supreme Court in *Serrano v. Priest* (1971) and of the United States Supreme Court in *San Antonio Independent School District v. Rodriguez* (1973).

8. *Minneapolis Tribune*, June 6, 1971, p. 4A.

9. Norton Long, "The City As Reservation," *The Public Interest* 25 (Fall 1971), 33.

10. George Sternleib, "The City as Sandbox," *The Public Interest* 25 (Fall, 1971).

11. The planner was Roger Starr. For some implications of this idea, see William Baer, "On the Death of Cities," *The Public Interest* 45 (Fall 1976).

12. Edward Brandt, *et. al.*, *The Plight of the Cities* (St. Paul: College of St. Thomas, 1972), p. 5.

13. See Committee for Economic Development, *Reshaping Governments in Metropolitan Areas* (New York: Committee for Economic Development, 1970).

14. See Advisory Commission on Intergovernmental Relations, *A Look to the North: Canadian Regional Experience*, Vol. V of *Substate Regionalism and the Federal System* (Washington, D.C.: U.S. Government Printing Office, 1973), Chapters 3 and 6.

15. Vincent L. Marando, "The Politics of Metropolitan Reform." In Alan K. Campbell and Roy W. Bahl, eds., *State and Local Government: The Political Economy of Reform* (New York: The Free Press, 1976), pp. 25-28.

16. Sharon P. Krefetz and Alan B. Sharof, "City-County Merger Attempts: The Role of Political Factors," *National Civic Review* (April 1977) p. 178.

17. Lowden Wingo, ed., *Reform of Metropolitan Governments* (Washington, D.C.: Resources for the Future, 1972), p. 1.

18. Scott Greer, *Metropolitics: A Study of Political Culture* (New York: Wiley, 1963).

19. On St. Louis see Robert H. Salisbury, "Interests, Parties, and Governmental Structures in St. Louis," *The Western Political Quarterly* 13, no. 2 (June 1960); Henry J. Schmandt, P. G. Steinbicker, and G. D. Wendel, *Metropolitan Reform in St. Louis* (New York: Holt, Rinehart and Winston, 1961). On Cleveland, see Estal E. Sparlin, "Cleveland Seeks New Metro Solution," *National Civic Review* 69, no. 3 (March 1960); James A. Norton, *The Metro Experience* (Cleveland: The Press of Western Reserve University, 1963); Richard A. Watson and John H. Romani, "Metropolitan Government for Metropolitan Cleveland: An Analysis of the Voting Record," *Midwest Journal of Political Science* 5, no. 4 (November 1961), pp. 365-90.

20. Marando, "The Politics of Metropolitan Reform," pp. 28-29.

21. Thomas A. Henderson and Walter A. Rosenbaum, "Prospects for Consolidation of Local Governments: The Role of Local Elites in Electoral Outcomes," *American Journal of Political Science* 17, no. 4 (November 1973), pp. 695-720.

22. James L. Sundquist, *Making Federalism Work* (Washington, D.C.: Brookings Institution, 1969), p. 1-6.

23. A decade later, scholars and political leaders began to worry that this interstate redistribution was draining the lifeblood out of the Northeast and Midwest states.

24. See *Minneapolis Tribune*, April 19, 1977.

25. Advisory Commission on Intergovernmental Relations, *Improving Federal Grants Management* (Washington, D.C.: 1977), pp. 216-17.

26. Melvin B. Mogulof, "Federally Encouraged Multi-Jurisdictional Agencies in Three Metropolitan Areas." In *Regional Governance: Promise and Performance*, Vol. II of *Substate Regionalism and the Federal System* (Washington, D.C.: U.S. Government Printing Office, 1973), p. 142.

Chapter 2

1. See Scott Greer, *Metropolitics: A Study of Political Culture* (New York: Wiley, 1963). On St. Louis see Henry J. Schmandt, P. G. Steinbicker, and G. D. Wendel, *Metropolitan Reform in St. Louis* (New York: Holt, Rinehart and Winston, 1961). On Cleveland, see James A. Norton, *The Metro Experience* (Cleveland: The Press of Western Reserve University, 1963).

2. Edward Brandt, *et. al.*, *The Plight of the Cities* (St. Paul: College of St. Thomas, 1972); *1973 Supplement to the Plight of the Cities* (St. Paul, College of St. Thomas, 1973).

3. On analyses of central city-suburban disparities, see Leo F. Schnore, "The Socio-Economic Status of Cities and Suburbs," *American Sociological Review* 38 (1963), pp. 122-34; John J. Harrigan, "A New Look at Central City-Suburban Differences," *Social Science* (Autumn, 1976).

4. For an excellent description of suburban growth patterns in the Twin Cities, see Ronald Abler, John S. Adams, and John R. Borchert, *The Twin Cities of St. Paul and Minneapolis* (Cambridge, Mass.: Ballinger Publishing Co., 1976), pp. 51-66.

5. Daniel J. Elazar, *American Federalism: A View from the States* (New York: Thomas Y. Crowell, 1966), pp. 89-97.

6. Jack L. Walker, "The Diffusion of Innovations among the American States," *American Political Science Review*, 63 (September 1969), pp. 880-99.

7. *Christian Science Monitor*, April 1, 1977, p. 35.

8. For background on the MPC, see Stanley Baldinger, *Planning and Governing the Metropolis: The Twin Cities Experience* (New York: Praeger, 1971), p. 63.

9. See Abler, Adams, and Borchert, *The Twin Cities*.

10. Vincent L. Marando and Carl Reggie Whitley, "City-County Consolidation: An overview of Voter Response," *Urban Affairs Quarterly* 8, no. 2 (December 1972), pp. 181-204, found that only nine of twenty-nine consolidation attempts were successful since 1945.

11. This sentiment was conveyed to the authors separately by Ted Kolderie in an interview August 9, 1977, and by the first Metropolitan Council chairman, James Hetland, Jr., in an interview August 10, 1977, Minneapolis, Minnesota.

12. Ted Kolderie, interview with William Johnson, May 28, 1976, Minneapolis, Minnesota. Ted Kolderie, interview with William Johnson and John Harrigan, August 9, 1977, Minneapolis, Minnesota.

13. Citizens League, "A Metropolitan Council for the Twin Cities Area," (Minneapolis, 1967).

14. For some examples of local governments paralyzing COGs, see: Frances Frisken, "The Metropolis and the Central City: Can One Government Unite Them?" *Urban Affairs Quarterly* 8, no. 3 (June 1973), pp. 395-422; Philip W. Barnes, *Metropolitan Coalitions: A Study of Councils of Government in Texas* (Austin: Institute of Public Affairs, University of Texas, 1969); Melvin B. Mogulof, *Governing Metropolitan Areas* (Washington, D.C.: The Urban Institute, 1971); Advisory Commission on Intergovernmental Relations, *Subregionalism Revisited: Recent Areawide and Local Responses* (Washington, D.C.: U.S. Government Printing Office, 1977), p. 24.

15. On incremental decision making, see David Braybrooke and Charles E. Lindblom, *A Strategy of Decision* (New York: Free Press, 1963), and Robert A. Dahl and Charles E. Lindblom, *Politics, Economics, and Welfare* (New York: Harper and Row, 1953).

16. On nonincremental decision making, see Paul Schulman, "Nonincremental Policy Making: Notes toward an Alternative Paradigm," *American Political Science Review* 69 (December 1975), pp. 1354-70.

17. Edward Knudson, *Regional Politics in the Twin Cities: A Report on the Politics and Planning of Urban Growth Policy* (St. Paul: Metropolitan Council, 1976), p. 34.

18. Ted Kolderie, "Governance in the Twin Cities Area of Minnesota." In *Regional Governance: Promise and Performance* (Washington, D.C.: Advisory Commission on Intergovernmental Relations, 1973), p. 118.

19. Knudson, *Regional Politics in the Twin Cities*, p. 38.

Chapter 3

1. *Minnesota Statutes* 473B.02, Subd. 4.

2. Metropolitan Council, *1976 Annual Report*, p. 3.

3. *Minnesota Statutes* 473.145.

4. Edward Knudson, *Regional Politics in the Twin Cities: A Report on the Politics and Planning of Urban Growth Policy* (St. Paul: Metropolitan Council, 1976), p. 22.

5. Metropolitan Council, *State of the Region* (St. Paul: Metropolitan Council, 1977), p. 113.

6. See John J. Harrigan, *Political Change in the Metropolis* (Boston: Little, Brown & Co., 1976), pp. 215-217.

7. *1976 Annual Report*, p. 5.

8. *Ibid.*, p. 12.

9. Harrigan, *Political Change in the Metropolis*, p. 400.

10. Calculated from tables in 1975 and 1976 *Annual Reports*.

11. In Michael E. Gleeson, "Selected Analyses of the Metropolitan Council as an Environmental Management Organization." In University of Minnesota School of Public Affairs, *Case Study of the Metropolitan Council as an Environmental Management Organization*, (Minneapolis, 1976), III, pp. 7-18, 42-44.

12. Peggy Reichert, *Growth Management in the Twin Cities Metropolitan Area: A Report for Planners on the Development Framework Planning Process* (St. Paul: The Metropolitan Council, 1976).

13. Roger Israel, "Preliminary Briefing Paper on A-95 in Relation to Social Framework" (Unpublished memorandum, November 18, 1976).

14. *Minneapolis Star*, September 25, 1976.

15. *1976 Annual Report*, p. 11.

16. See Frances Frisken, "The Metropolis and the Central City: Can One Government Unite Them?" *Urban Affairs Quarterly* 8, no. 3 (June 1973); and Philip W. Barnes, *Metropolitan Coalitions: A Study of Councils of Government in Texas* (Austin: Institute of Public Affairs, University of Texas, 1969).

Chapter 4

1. Metropolitan Health Board, *Health Systems Plan for the Metropolitan Area*, draft for public hearing, April 14, 1977. Policy 14, p. 20.

2. Metropolitan Council, "Development Framework Chapter," *Metropolitan Develop-*

ment Guide, draft for public hearings, January 1975; p. vi states "This chapter supersedes the February 25, 1971, Major Diversified Centers chapter."

3. See Morton Grodzins, "The Federal System." In the President's Commission on National Goals, *Goals for Americans* (Englewood Cliffs, N.J.: Prentice-Hall, 1960), p. 265.

4. Deil S. Wright, "Intergovernmental Relations: An Analytic Overview," *The Annals of the American Academy of Political and Social Science*, (November 1974), p. 15.

5. On the concept of functional fiefdoms, see John J. Harrigan, *Political Change in the Metropolis* (Boston: Little, Brown & Co., 1976), Chapter 5.

6. "Development Framework Chapter," p. 2.

7. *Ibid.*, p. 29.

8. This criticism was made emphatically by three of the persons interviewed by the authors. Also see Citizens League, *Balancing the New Use and Re-Use of Land* (Minneapolis, Minn.: Citizens League, January 26, 1976). For the Metropolitan Council's major response see Fully Developed Area Task Force, *A New Urban Policy* (St. Paul, Minn: The Metropolitan Council, April 1977).

9. *Agricultural Planning Handbook: Identifying Long-Term Productive Land* (St. Paul: The Metropolitan Council, July 1976).

10. For a fuller discussion of the Development Framework and its implementation, see Oliver Byrum and Robert Hoffman, "Development Framework Guide, Regional Land Use, Public Facilities," *Practicing Planner*, 7, no. 1 (March 1977), pp. 20-28.

11. Metropolitan Council, "Waste Management Chapter," *Metropolitan Development Guide*, adopted September 25, 1975, p. iii.

12. *Ibid.*, pp. 20-22.

13. *Ibid.*, p. iii.

14. Maurice Dotten, interview with John Harrigan, July 19, 1977, St. Paul, Minnesota.

15. Metropolitan Council, "Transportation Guide/Policy Plan Chapter," *Metropolitan Development Guide*, adopted 1976, p. 10.

16. *Minneapolis Tribune*, August 17, 1977, p. A-1.

17. *St. Paul Dispatch*, July 17, 1977.

18. See K. H. Schaeffer and Elliott Sclar, *Access for All: Transportation and Urban Growth* (Baltimore, Md.: Penguin Books, 1975), pp. 63-79.

19. Metropolitan Council, "Recreation Open Space Development Guide-Policy Plan Chapter," *Metropolitan Development Guide*, adopted December 19, 1974, p. 15.

20. *Ibid.*

21. See Metropolitan Council, *Monthly Review*, June 1977.

22. *Metropolitan Investment Framework*, Draft III, March 24, 1977, p. 12.

23. Ronald Abler, John S. Adams, and John R. Borchert, *The Twin Cities of St. Paul and Minneapolis* (Cambridge, Mass.: Ballinger Publishing Co., 1976), p. 49.

24. *Metropolitan Investment Framework*, p. 12.

25. *Ibid.*, p. 18.

26. *Ibid.*, p. 24.

Chapter 5

1. Metropolitan Council, "Solid Waste Management Policies, System Plan, Program Chapter," *Metropolitan Development Guide*, adopted March 12, 1970, p. 4.

2. *Ibid.*, p. 4.

3. *Ibid.*, p. 17.

4. *Ibid.*, p. 14.

5. Metropolitan Council, *Policies for Resource Recovery Facilities — Amendments to the Metropolitan Development Guide on Solid Waste Management*, (November 1976), p. 1.

6. *Ibid.*, p. 12.

7. *Ibid.*

8. Maurice Dotten, interview with John Harrigan, July 19, 1977, St. Paul, Minnesota.

9. "Waste Management Chapter," *Metropolitan Development Guide*, 1975, p. 13.

10. *Ibid.*, p. 13.

11. Metropolitan Council, "Water Resources Policy Plan, Program Chapter," *Metropolitan Development Guide*, adopted August 9, 1973, p. xii.

12. Marcel R. Jouseau, "Regional Approach to Groundwater Management in the Twin Cities." In *Proceedings of the 8th Annual Water Resources Seminar Groundwater Resources and Development*, November 24 and 25, 1975, at the Water Resources Research Center, University of Minnesota (Minneapolis: University of Minnesota, Water Resources Center, May 1976), pp. 43-44.

13. "Water Resources Policy Plan, Program Chapter," *Metropolitan Development Guide*, p. 85.

14. *Ibid.*, p. 3.

15. Metropolitan Council, "Protection Open Space Policy Plan, Program Chapter," *Metropolitan Development Guide*, adopted April 26, 1973, pp. 1-17.

16. *Ibid.*, p. 4.

17. *Ibid.*, p. 8.

18. Jouseau, "Regional Approach to Groundwater Management in the Twin Cities," pp. 42-43.

19. Metropolitan Council, *Model Ordinances for Environmental Protection* (St. Paul, March 1977).

20. Marcel Jouseau, interview with John Harrigan, July 22, 1977, St. Paul, Minnesota.

21. See *Minneapolis Tribune*, October 25, 1976, p. 14-A.

22. Metropolitan Council, *State of the Region*, (St. Paul: Metropolitan Council, 1977), pp. 47-53.

23. Fully Developed Area Task Force, *A New Urban Policy* (St. Paul: Metropolitan Council, 1977), p. 73.

24. See Metropolitan Council, *A Fair Share Plan*, April 1977.

25. *Minneapolis Star*, July 21, 1977, p. 4-B.

26. Health Board of the Metropolitan Council, *Health Systems Plan for the Metropolitan Area: Metropolitan Development Guide*. Draft for public hearing, April 14, 1977.

27. *Ibid.*, p. 58.

28. *Ibid.*, "Introduction of the Metropolitan Health Board," April 5, 1976; available from the Health Board of the Metropolitan Council, St. Paul, Minnesota 55101.

29. Malcolm Mitchell, interview with John Harrigan, July 21, 1977, St. Paul, Minnesota.

30. Jane Whitesides, "The Council's Role in Aging," *Perspectives* (October-December, 1976), p. 4.

31. Metropolitan Council, *1976 Annual Report*, pp. 7, 28-29.

Chapter 6

1. Council of Metropolitan Area Leagues, League of Women Voters of Minnesota, *Survey of Attitudes toward the Metropolitan Council*, (St. Paul, 1976).

2. Vern Peterson, interview with William Johnson and John Harrigan, July 29, 1977. St. Paul, Minnesota.

3. Michael E. Gleeson, "Selected Analyses of the Metropolitan Council as an Environmental Management Organization," University of Minnesota School of Public Affairs, *Case Study of the Metropolitan Council as an Environmental Management Organization* (Minneapolis, 1976), pp. iii-42.

4. *Ibid.*, p. 41.

5. See, for example, David Easton, *The Political System*, 2nd ed., (New York: Alfred A. Knopf, 1971) p. 129.

6. *Regional Politics in the Twin Cities* (St. Paul: The Metropolitan Council, 1976), p. v.

7. Vern Peterson, interview.

8. Advisory Commission on Intergovernmental Relations, *Regionalism Revisitied: Recent Areawide and Local Responses* (Washington, D.C.: U.S. Government Printing Office, 1977), p. 23.

9. Fully Developed Area Task Force, *A New Urban Policy* (St. Paul: Metropolitan Council, 1977).

10. This research has most recently been published in Commission on Minnesota's Future, *Report* (St. Paul, 1977); Upper Midwest Council, *Emerging Forces in Conflict* (Minneapolis, 1977); and Minnesota State Planning Agency, Office of the State Demographer, *Faces of the Future* (St. Paul, 1977).

11. Metropolitan Council, *Population Projections, 1977.*

12. *Faces of the Future*, p. 21.

13. *Ibid.*, pp. 27-30.

14. See, for example, Jon Shafer, "The Impact of New Technologies and Life Styles on Urban Development," unpublished manuscript, n.d. (Shafer was communications program manager for the Metropolitan Council.)

15. Grover Starling, "Political Implications of a Look-Out Institution," *Futures* 5 (October 1973), pp. 484-90.

16. Commission on Minnesota's Future, *Report*, p. 54.

17. Ronald Abler, John S. Adams, and John R. Borchert, *The Twin Cities of St. Paul and Minneapolis* (Cambridge, Mass.: Ballinger Publishing Co., 1976) pp. 43-50.

18. *A New Urban Policy*, p. 73.

19. One of the most thoughtful discussions of the elective Metropolitan Council issue is that of Robert Einsweiler, "Thoughts about an Elected vs. Appointed Metropolitan Council," *Perspectives* 2 (April-June 1977) pp. 4-7.

20. Ted Smebakken, interview with William Johnson and John Harrigan, August 17, 1977, St. Paul, Minnesota.

21. University of Minnesota School of Public Affairs, *Case Study of the Metropolitan Council*, p. I-34.

22. University of Minnesota School of Public Affairs, *Planning and Development Management System for the Twin Cities Metropolitan Area* (Minneapolis, 1973-74) p. II-19.

23. Vern Peterson, interview.

24. *Planning and Development Management System for the Twin Cities Metropolitan Area*, p. II-19.

25. See Thomas M. Scott, "The Diffusion of Urban Governmental Forms as a Case of Social Learning," *Journal of Politics* 30 (November 1968) pp. 1091-1109; and Jack L. Walker, "The Diffusion of Innovations among the American States," *American Political Science Review* 63 (September 1969) pp. 880-99.

26. *Regionalism Revisited*, pp. 24-25.

27. Ted Kolderie, "The 'Process' Used Here Is What Should Be Copied," *Citizens League News*, November 30, 1976, p. 4.

28. On the Citizens League's activities, see Chapter 2 this volume or Ted Kolderie and Paul Gilje, "The Citizens League," *National Civic Review* 65, no. 7 (July 1976), pp. 322-42.

Index

Index